Get Happy NOW!

Get Happy in 10 Minutes.
Feel Happy in 10 Days.
Be Happy for Life!

Also by Joseph McClendon III, Ph.D.

Unlimited Power: A Black Choice
(co-author with Anthony Robbins)

*Ebony Power Thoughts: Inspirational Thoughts
from Outstanding African Americans*
(co-author with Anthony Robbins)

Change Your Breakfast, Change Your Life

Praise for Joseph McClendon III, Ph.D.

"I have seen many speakers, but I can say without a second thought Joseph definitely put the dots on the I's and the cross on my T's of life. In a nutshell, the guy makes you do it."

    —Jane Prior, Senior Executive, Slim It Gyms, Inc.

"Without doubt Joseph changed my whole focus. He is a 21st century motivator; his knowledge is so today, so powerful, yet so necessary. I suggest that anybody with a need to step up in their lives should make Joseph a must-see."

    —John Miller, M.D., Circular Securities

"Step by step, Joseph McClendon, in his fun and powerful style, shows how to reprogram the mind in minutes, how to blast through obstacles and turn them into opportunities, and how to resolve internal conflicts so you are assured of success."

    —Lynn Rose

"It truly is amazing how Joseph works. He really understands people. He knows exactly how and where to get you started, how to finish, and most of all how to really enjoy the journey along the way."

    —Tianna DeGuire, wellness coach

"When I first met Joseph I was 19 years old. I was labeled severe ADD, I was on a lot of medication, and I felt like I was never going to have a normal life. Now, I'm on the front cover of bicycle magazines, I own my own business, and I feel absolutely fantastic."

    —Kevin Westin, downhill bicycle racer

"Whether it's a housewife working with her children, or somebody who wants to take it up to the next level in their company or business, or someone who just wants to be a better person, by following Joseph's simple plan of being able to grow yourself first, everything else in life will simply follow."

—Jeff Vindetti, international business owner

"There is no question that Joseph will shift your thinking and change your life. That's a given. The real value is in the processional effect that it will have on you, family, friends and virtually everyone who you love and interact with. It's truly a lifelong gift."

—Andy Broadaway, Owner & CEO, The Tube Doctor

"I can tell you that Joseph has changed my life in some critical ways. I really didn't have a strong belief system and I was able to borrow his. What is amazing is it allowed me to move toward my future in a very positive way and to handle challenges much more easily in my life."

—Dean Shafer, CEO, International Wellness Center

Get Happy NOW!

Get Happy in 10 Minutes.
Feel Happy in 10 Days.
Be Happy for Life!

by Joseph McClendon III, Ph.D.

SUCCESS

Published by SUCCESS®, a SUCCESS Partners Company.

SUCCESS®

200 Swisher Road
Lake Dallas, Texas 75065
Toll-free: 866-SUCCESS (782-2377)
www.SUCCESS.com

Printed in the United States of America.

Book design by Alan Dwelle and Sam Watson
Cover design by Greg Luther

ISBN 978-1-935944-54-6

SPECIAL SALES
SUCCESS Books are available at special discounts for bulk purchase for sales promotions and premiums. Special editions, including personalized covers, excerpts of existing books, and corporate imprints, can be created in large quantities for special needs. For more information, contact Special Markets, SUCCESS, sales@success.com.

*"Happiness is the meaning and the purpose of life,
the whole aim and end of human existence."*

—*Aristotle*

This book is dedicated to the most important Josephs in my life.

To my father, Joseph McClendon Jr.: Papa, your love and life lessons define who I have been.

To my beautiful son, Joseph McClendon IV: You define who I shall become. Your smiles make me happiest of all.

Contents

Is it possible to prescribe happiness?

After decades of working with individuals across the globe in the area of life transformation, I can attest that one of the biggest underlying desires of human beings is to be happy and that happiness can, in fact, be learned. Nobody wants a future filled with anguish, sadness, sorrow, and self-pity. In our ideal dreams we imagine ourselves laughing, loving, grateful, and full of hope.

Happiness, like success, is a choice. It's a choice to listen, learn, and execute the wisdom of those who can help you become who you want to be. It's a process, but it's the greatest investment you can make. It's your life.

Joseph McClendon III has been a friend and colleague for more than two and a half decades, speaking on stage at my events, training my trainers and transforming lives along the way. He's one of the happiest guys I know, and he walks the talk. He's a joy anchor for me and my wife and for countless others in this world. Whenever I see that I have an email from Joseph in my inbox, I smile because nine times out of ten it will make me laugh out loud. Joseph isn't just another self-help guru trying to make a name for himself. In addition to his uncanny ability to bring out the joy and happiness in himself and others, he is a skilled technician in the field of human transformation and the neurosciences. He is compassionate, yet direct, and truly loves life and cares about people.

Joseph has a process that works.

He understands human psychology and man's search for meaning, which is as old as the beginning of time. Aristotle said, *Happiness depends upon ourselves.* That was three thousand years ago. Today, mankind still has a burning desire to understand the meaning of life and the quest for happiness. How do we achieve it? How does one get what they want? How can we become happier, wealthier, healthier, and more successful?

Is it possible to rewire your brain to "learn" how to be happy? Science says yes. Studies have emerged from the psychology and neuroscience fields that prove that we have greater control over our own individual happiness than we might have thought possible. It IS possible to learn a method that will help you rewire your brain, and continually make the right choices.

My deepest wish for you is that you find and keep a friend like Joseph and that you take what you are about to learn and enhance your life and the lives of the ones you love and care about.

Congratulations on your choice to begin this journey.

Anthony Robbins
Entrepreneur, author and peak-performance strategist
www.tonyrobbins.com

Science has proven what most of us have already suspected.

You've known it your entire life. Happy people live longer. They're healthier, more energetic, more fun to be around, and they draw you in to their vibrant personalities like a moth to a flame.

Now, scientific studies across the world have documented this truth. Research on centenarians (people who live to be over 100) report commonalities such as high levels of self-esteem, a connectedness to others, and a happy countenance. Why is being happy so important? Because it's your life.

Happiness has been the subject of study in universities, think tanks, corporations, and organizations across the globe. Millions of dollars have been spent studying the pursuit, and end result, of living a happier life. It's no longer hearsay, or conjecture. It's not a bunch of positive thinking mumbo jumbo taught by crystal-wearing California woo-woo, hippy throwbacks from the 1960s. It's not unproven pop psychology delivered by the latest guru, or shortcut media hype aimed at selling books or seminars. It's hard-core, proven science, based on two decades of meticulously documented research, intense clinical study, experimentation, and consistent results.

Happy people live longer, love better, and have more success. And the simple beauty is that a happier, healthier life IS attainable, if you choose to embrace it.

Notice I didn't say chase it.

Happiness can be (and is) taught. You can read this book and learn how to create a happier, richer life, right now. Together, we can center happiness at the core of your existence like the hub of a wheel, so that every other aspect of your life is a spoke stemming from that hub. In doing so you will not only forever alter the course of your own life but also impact the lives of all you have the privilege of influencing.

That's right; your ability to sustain happiness is directly, radically, and permanently connected to every aspect of your life. It affects your health, wealth, relationships, and even your ability to attract abundance. It's not a replacement for God, spirituality, or any of those things. It's a necessity. Like water or oxygen, it's a fundamental element of life that so many humans are missing.

Getting happy is not the problem. I can (and will) show you how to do that in an instant. It's staying happy long enough to make it a natural default in your nervous system that's the key to bringing about true, lasting, sustainable happiness and all of its benefits. Even if you create or manufacture happiness you can cause your nervous system to automatically return to happiness more often than not. And the great news is that you already do this with virtually every habit, skill, and behavior in your entire life. I'm just going to show you how to do it with happiness.

We each desire happiness. But at times it seems impossible to find. How do I know it? I know because I was once the unhappiest man on the planet. I've traveled a journey from broke and homeless to healthy, wealthy, and happy beyond belief. But this isn't a book about material wealth. It's a book about your own internal wealth and the strengths and resources and gifts you have to make the world a better place. And the material wealth will flow to you as a result.

What This Book Is About

I'm going to show you how everything you do is connected to your level of consistent happiness. *This is a book about you.*

Your life is an amazing testimony to what any human can achieve, and if I or anyone can do it, you can too! Whether you're a CEO of a multinational corporation or the barista at your local Starbucks, it makes no difference. I'm going to show you step by step how to cultivate, grow, and sustain your own personal happiness in a way that it becomes a natural extension of who you really are.

Anything is possible! You may have picked up this book out of sheer curiosity. You may be having the best time of your life and you want to know why, and how to sustain it. Or maybe you're having the worst time of your life and can't seem to dig yourself out of a rut. Perhaps you're just searching for something more in your career, relationships, and friends, or maybe you want what you want sooner rather than later.

No matter who you are, where you are in life, or what you do, you CAN learn how to be happy. And by the way, I'm not just talking about that obnoxious, polished exterior show of happiness that has all the earmarks of a borderline schizophrenic. I'm talking about real, unshakable happiness to the core. The kind that even when the worst happens, there's something inside that is cemented in a certainty that everything is going to work out fine. The kind that makes you get up early and stay up late. The passion that makes time fly because you're having so much fun doing what you're doing, and people and things fly to you.

So hang on tight. You're in for the ride of your life! Put your seat back and tray table in their upright position because we're headed on a journey that will transform you, your family, and the world around you.

Chapter 1

LIFE IS MUCH SIMPLER THAN YOU'VE BEEN LED TO BELIEVE

"Every morning in Africa, a gazelle wakes up. It knows it must outrun the fastest lion or it will be killed. Every morning in Africa, a lion wakes up. It knows it must run faster than the slowest gazelle, or it will starve. It doesn't matter whether you're a lion or a gazelle—when the sun comes up, you'd better be running."
—Abe Gubegan, Ethiopian journalist

The beginning is always magnificent.

From the very moment you come kicking and screaming into this world you have just three constant needs and one fear. These components accompany all of us throughout our entire lives and shape our destiny along the way. The needs are: to avoid pain, to pursue pleasure, and to grow and learn. The fear is the fear of abandonment and being left alone. Each one feeds on the others, forming a complex set of behaviors and personality traits. That, mixed with an endless combination of life experiences, helps make us who we are. But where do you go from here?

Inside of you is a seed of greatness beckoning you to make a difference in the world. A desire to be content, happy, and to live an abundant life. You've already achieved so much. So what prevents you from living full on, in ultimate happiness? Why do we fall short of consistent peace, joy, and thrilling excitement, in favor of allowing external circumstances to dictate our lives?

When I first sat down to write this book I couldn't escape the feeling of gratitude that my life had come full circle. At one point I was literally face down in the mud, homeless, and living in a cardboard box. Now I'm speaking, writing books, coaching celebrities and running $20 million companies. Bigger than that is the privilege of being able to give back and impact lives.

As I look at my own life, I'm humbled and grateful for the blessings that have come my way. My health, my body, and my mind are functioning better than they did when in my thirties. Aside from having been called the happiest guy on the planet, I've taught thousands of people to live their dreams. I'm passionate about teaching others how to have what I have: a positive, joyful outlook, and in twenty-five years of practice and presenting to over three million people around the globe, I have witnessed what I can only describe as astounding behavior in my fellow man. I've seen men and women who have everything they could ever want walk around miserable, sad, depressed, and unhappy. And I've seen others who have next to nothing and no means of getting even sustenance for the next day being joyful, happy, cheerful, and full of hope. I have also seen just the opposite and virtually every variation in between.

I wrote this book for you. If you're not living in ultimate joy, you should be. If ever there were a time to be happy, it's right the hell now. Unless you have been living under a rock you know that globally we are undergoing some challenging times in terms of optimism, hope, and faith. Not to mention economically, culturally with regard to tolerance and globalism, and health, to name just a few. Even if you are one of the estimated three and one-half percent of the people on the planet who truly are happy, positive, and optimistic, now is the time to pay it forward.

Today I'm an ultimate performance specialist and I speak all over the world, helping audiences and individuals grow and transform. But it wasn't always that way.

We've all had times in our lives when we felt defeated and unappreciated. Times when the struggle to keep our attitude above the plumb line was difficult and unlikely. Situations and circumstances that seemed unfair, unjust, and even directed at you personally as though you carried some sort of bad luck mojo or there was a target on your back. Even though trying times may feel like they last an eternity and seem insurmountable, they always pass. And when they do, you've got to evolve into a better you, instead of going backward.

A Crossroads Moment

I can look back briefly to reflect on the day I had a serious awakening. Have you ever had a crossroads moment? That's the one where you realize you're in that space between who you once were, and who you are about to become. I had my moment, and I remember it like it was yesterday, though I'm not that person anymore.

The tears were frozen on the side of my face, because I had been weeping for 75 miles. As I crossed the double yellow line and pulled out into the oncoming traffic lane, my mind raced with a mixture of fear and self-pity and I knew I couldn't go on any longer. I had reached the end. Literally. The pain in my soul was so loud and deep that it made me scream at the top of my lungs. In an effort to hasten the end I twisted the throttle wide open on my dilapidated 1937 Harley-Davidson. I wanted to go out in a blaze of glory. Well, okay, cowardly stupidity.

Seventy, 80, 95, 100 miles an hour… I pushed that tired old engine beyond the limit. That bike was my pride and joy, and along with about eight dollars and the clothes on my back, was all

I owned.

It was the eve of my 19th birthday. Other guys my age were just starting their lives, had girlfriends, jobs, or attended college, but I was stuck in despair and negative thinking. I felt so small, as if I was meaningless. And for several months I had been on a destructive, downward spiral. I was broke and homeless, living in a cardboard box behind the Antelope Valley Drive-in Theater in Lancaster, California. I was too embarrassed to tell my friends and family I was living a lie, so instead of asking for help, I would act as if everything was normal and retreat to my horrible cardboard hellhole out in the pitch black of the cold Mojave Desert.

Earlier that day I had driven to another small desert town, Ridgecrest, California, where my mother lived. Although I went there under the guise of visiting her because it was my birthday, the truth of the matter was I knew that she would feed me a good meal and give me a few dollars. She was like that. Even though she didn't have much, she would always slip ten dollars in my pocket and never take no for an answer. I had planned on staying for a few days to have a warm pillow to lay my head on. But my last shred of dignity was torn away when she asked me how I was doing and I lied to her.

"Fine," I said.

I told her that I was doing well and was working, and I even said I was back in school and had an apartment. The words fell like stones from my lips, and I felt a piece of my soul decaying. I could no longer look her in the eyes! I was too ashamed to tell her the truth, but it was the lie that bothered me even more than the reality of how little I had achieved. To me I could get no lower than lying to my mother. So I left shortly after that conversation, feeling sadder than ever.

During the hour and a half drive on my way home, I knew that I had reached the end. I couldn't go any further down. I had lied to the one person who loved me most.

It seemed like there was nothing to live for. No future, no relationship, no career. Perhaps the worst of it was I had no coping mechanism for getting out of my mental torture. I was not happy! And worse than just that, my unhappiness had caused me to believe that was who I was, versus just a moment in time. My depressed state had made me think that I would never be happy. I thought my life was over, and on that long drive home, I contemplated how I would finally do it. I was speeding through traffic driving my motorcycle as fast as it would go, distraught and full of jumbled, complex thoughts, with tears running down my face.

When I saw the headlights coming, it occurred to me that I could swerve the bike into the path of the vehicle and in one second my pain would be over. I was screaming at the top of my lungs. I'm not sure what I was screaming but it felt like it was coming from my very soul. At the peak of my hysteria, I heard my mother's voice...

"You never hurt another human being."

Her voice was crystal clear, as if she were there with me. It was something she had said to me many times. She always told me you never ever hurt another person on this planet, you help them. And it struck me like lightning. I am another person! Not to mention that I could hurt someone else by doing something selfish and stupid. So at the last second I swerved back into my lane. I just kept driving on autopilot, even more distraught. Here I was, with absolutely nothing to live for, and I couldn't even kill myself. I felt totally worthless. I remember thinking to myself "It can't get any worse than this."

But seconds later, it did get worse. In that moment when I was drowning in my own self-pity and worthlessness, a semi in front of me blew a tire. I looked up and saw a large piece of rubber in the air.

Talk about an immediate shift in perspective!

Seconds before, I wanted to die. But now I had no choice and

I watched in horror as a 100-pound chunk of flying, jettisoned rubber propelled backward toward my head. A part of me welcomed the irony and an end to my pain, so I braced for the impact. But instinctively my physical reflexes kicked in and I ducked. The chunk missed my head but it hit me in the shoulder and knocked me off my bike. The impact sent me cartwheeling into the desert, the bike crashing and scattering parts, my body broken like a rag doll. I felt my insides bursting and bones breaking each time I hit the frozen desert floor, blood spurting from my wounds. The last thing I remember seeing was my precious hog tumbling end over end, engine racing and headlight flickering out.

Life has a way of shaking you up.

When I woke up it was dark, and I was all alone. My first realization was that no one had stopped to help me. But I didn't remain stuck in that thought. I kept moving. It was just me out there, and the mangled piece of metal that used to be my only possession. I walked back and found my motorcycle crumpled and bent. I reached over and pulled it up but in distress I didn't know what else to do so I pushed my broken bike the final ten miles back to my cardboard house. It was about 11 at night, and I still remember my thought, which was; well it can't get any worse than this. But guess what? It did!

At that moment it started raining.

It never rains in the desert.

I began crying like a little baby, as I watched the rain running like a river through my homeless camp, flooding everything. I lost it. As far as I'm concerned I flipped out with nowhere left to go! I began screaming, out loud.

"This will change, right now!"

"This will change, right now!"

"This will change, right now!"

My tears were mixed with anger and frustration.

Then I looked down at my watch in the darkness, and suddenly the moon hit it in just the right way so I could view the time. But my watch had stopped. The hands weren't working anymore, and it was frozen.

It had stopped at midnight.

Suddenly it dawned on me; "I'm 19 years old," I thought, remembering my birthday. Literally, I just turned 19, and in my mind 19 meant that you were a man. I don't know why but I snapped and started screaming again. Like a crazy lunatic I began yelling.

"I'm a man!"

"I'm a man!"

"I'm a man!"

It occurred to me that I was a man now, and there was no way to continue to fail, and do childish things. That's not what a man does. I continued yelling until I fell asleep in the mud. Little did I know that, during that evening with my behavior and my thought processes, I had stumbled upon the beginnings of rewiring my brain for happiness.

On the morning of the first day of my nineteenth year, I felt different. Even though I can intellectualize it now, I didn't know why at the time. Inside I knew that things were going to change for the better. Nothing in my life had changed regarding my situation, but I was feeling the seeds of happiness and hopefulness. I pushed my motorcycle out into the road and immediately saw a sign for a welding shop. I couldn't believe my eyes! It gave me hope.

I had lived in that town many years and had never seen it before, but there, right in front of my eyes, was a welding shop. It was still quite early but I could tell that someone was in there so I knocked on the door. An elderly man dressed in bib overalls and a wrinkled plaid shirt cracked open the door. He took one look at my muddy, bloody, pathetic ass and visibly scowled.

"What the hell do you want? There ain't nothing for you here."

I explained to him what had happened and proposed that I

could be of service to him by cleaning his shop or sweeping the floors or any kind of work he had for me if he would just weld my motorcycle frame.

"Today is my birthday and today I'm a man," I announced.

Instead of the look of compassion I was hoping for he looked at me like I was trash. "Like I said, there ain't nothing here for you, now get!"

He slammed the door in my face and I could hear him grumbling as he walked away. Much to my own surprise, instead of getting angry or hurt it struck me as a challenge. Even a bit funny. For some reason I thought to myself, *I'm a man now and a man never takes no for an answer.* So I knocked on the door again. This time when he came to the door he was genuinely pissed. I could see fire in his eyes. Before he could speak up I said, "Look, I know I must look like hell but I am determined to prove to you that I can help you and if you give me a chance you won't be sorry."

He looked at me, and then glanced at my broken mess of a bike in the driveway. Then back at me. After what seemed like an eternity he finally said. "The only reason I'm going to help you is because I used to have an old knucklehead like that one back in the day."

I pushed my bike into his garage and he gave me some clean clothes and told me to go in the back and clean myself up. When I returned he was sitting behind his cluttered desk in his junky, grease-smeared office.

"Sit down," he barked. "Before I lift one finger to fix your hog you are going to read this book cover to cover."

He threw a small paperback book at me and I caught it as I fell back into the rickety old armchair. At first I was scared and wondered what the hell I had gotten myself into. I remember thinking, *Just fix the bike! I don't like to read!*

The old man sensed my irritation. "Look," he said. "The garage is locked and the only way to get the bike is to read this book."

Now I was fuming. How dare he!

But when I looked at the book something changed. I knew I had reached a crossroads. It was worn out and dog-eared and there was no front or back cover. The book was *Think and Grow Rich* by Napoleon Hill.

I read that book in one day (because I wanted my bike), but you know what? I couldn't put it down. The concepts within it set the foundation for how I moved forward. The book changed my life forever and ignited a fire inside. Within a week I had a job, and a new attitude. I'd changed. For real.

The old man and I became friends and until his passing ten years ago we stayed in touch. The gift he gave me was priceless but he gave me an even bigger gift. When I went back and asked him how I could repay him for what he did for me (because he never even let me clean his shop), this is what he told me.

"You must do the same for others that I have done for you."

And that's the reason I do what I do to this day.

It's amazing to me even today that the legacy of one man could effect change in my life, and cascade downward to affect the lives of so many others. Napoleon Hill lived from October 26, 1883 to November 8, 1970. He was an author whose best-selling book was one of the greatest books of all time (at the time of Hill's death, *Think and Grow Rich* had sold 20 million copies).

Hill became an advisor to President Franklin D. Roosevelt, but he also is famous for his work with Andrew Carnegie, who asked Hill to interview top millionaires to determine the secret to their success. Today, this might be commonplace but imagine the impact of it back then. As part of his research, Hill interviewed many of the most famous people of the time, including Thomas Edison, Alexander Graham Bell, George Eastman, Henry Ford, John D. Rockefeller Sr., Charles M. Schwab, F.W. Woolworth, William Wrigley, Theodore Roosevelt, William H. Taft, and others. As a result, the *Philosophy of Achievement* was offered as a formula for rags-to-riches success by Hill and Carnegie, published as a course called *The Law of Success*. All of that research and self-improvement observation kicked off a study of the human psyche that has grown into a massive industry. We are still quoting Carnegie today, and still reading Hill's amazing book, *Think and Grow Rich*. And this, my friend, is the power of legacy. It's the purpose for all we do.

Legacy is the intellectual property you will pass on to the next generation. It's the wisdom and knowledge your children and grandchildren will glean from you, and your actions either seen or unseen. *What's your legacy going to be?*

This is how I know that total life transformation is possible in a short amount of time.

I've had high highs, and low lows, but I don't let either define me. And yes, I've been wealthy and wildly successful in finances, but that's not what this is all about. It's about developing yourself into the person you know you were meant to be, and living the life of your dreams.

Though the book was and still is magnificent, it was just my starting point of a lifelong fascination with human behavior and function. I went on to study psychology in college and eventually earned my doctorate in neuropsychology. I opened a practice in Los Angeles and have had the honor and privilege of assisting hundreds of individuals quickly alleviate the emotional and behavioral challenges that have impeded their lives. I've been there. The road to happiness is both legitimate and systematic.

A Prescription for Happiness

See, the world of self-help gurus and experts might make it seem like there's a fourteen-step process for everything, but I'm going to let you in on a little secret right upfront: *life is much simpler than that.* It's not as hard to change as you think it is, and that's why I want to give you a formula for happiness that works—now, next week, and for life.

Each day can be filled with an unimaginable, contagious, crazy joy, if you're willing to take the steps!

When you're rich, (in mind, body, and soul) and happy, you're going to be a different person than you are right now. I'm going to give you a new way to think.

Chapter 2

TRANSFORM

"To achieve your goals, make the right thing easy to do."
—Dr. Oz

» **HAVE FUN!**

» **ENGAGE IN THE PROCESS**

» **BELIEVE IN YOUR SUCCESS**

» **CHANGE YOUR BRAIN, CHANGE YOUR LIFE**

Your brain will change when you read this book.

Literally.

The human brain has 100 billion neurons, and each time you learn something new your brain generates new ones. This growth can continue as you age, contributing to your happiness, health, and longevity. In new brain research neurobiologists have been able to observe neurons through a video microscope as they grow and form new dendrites. This research is groundbreaking because it shatters the prior belief doctors held that, as we age, brain cells die and cannot regenerate.

Scientists studying the growth of new neurons in the brain know that the brain can in fact rewire itself, and that certain regions remain highly dynamic throughout life. Dr. Gage, a scientist at the Salk Institute, led a team that took postmortem brain tissue from patients, while other researchers viewed cells under various microscopes to determine that brain cells can in fact regenerate. Talk about transformation!

It's a Myth That You Can't Teach an Old Dog New Tricks

Your brain can stay young. And a huge key to keeping it that way is to be intentional about exercising it. When you focus on transforming thoughts and increase (in any area of your life), the result is a positive flow into every area of your life. It's like turning on a water faucet. Transformation leads to multiplication.

No matter what your age, researchers have proven that you can change your brain, and change your life. You can learn a new skill, hobby, or profession. But did you know that it's also possible to learn how to be happier?

This is your moment. Transformation is in the air, and the path beyond it contains the fully engaged, full on, abundantly joyful life where you have exceedingly more.

How to Get the Absolute Most Out of This Book

Engage in the process!

This book is a living tool. It's based on decades of research, but more important, on the most recent advances in brain psychology and neurosciences. Brain research is rapidly evolving, exploding and dispelling old beliefs! How cool that doctors who once believed the brain couldn't regenerate itself now know the truth: your brain cells can be regenerated, and you can grow healthy new ones, if you (literally) put your mind to it.

To produce the results you want you must engage and interact. Consider the man who prayed to the Lord every day for 30 years that he might win the lottery. When he passed away without ever winning he said, "Lord, I was a good man, an honest man, a good husband, and a great father. I read my Bible every day and went to church every Sunday. Lord, you know that I prayed every day to win the lottery yet you let me pass away without ever winning. Why Lord? Why didn't you ever answer my prayers?"

The Lord said, "You never bought a lottery ticket."

NO MATTER WHAT YOUR AGE, RESEARCHERS HAVE PROVEN THAT YOU CAN CHANGE YOUR BRAIN, AND CHANGE YOUR LIFE.

Dr. Oz, the television host, friend of Oprah and famous surgeon, wrote that change is possible, but only if you believe it. You must participate in your own rise to greatness. When you do you'll become like a magnet to the people, places, and things that you desire along the way. Said differently—you will go further faster. Throughout this book I will be asking you to do certain things. Write things down, think about things and even move your body in certain ways. Each of these exercises has a specific reason and purpose, and they are in a certain sequence. Each step is designed to build on the previous one.

Although I will be explaining a great deal of the process and how it works, please know that it is not necessary for you to understand everything for it to work. As a matter of fact, in a great deal of the cases the less you try to understand it the faster you will affect your nervous system and your subconscious mind. Kind of like the exercise in the movie the *Karate Kid* where the young boy is put through the paces of a repetitive wax on, wax off process by his mentor. If you've ever seen the film, you'll recall that the young boy was extremely frustrated and angry by his karate instructor asking him to perform mindless exercises and tasks. He wanted to fight, but the instructor had him stand in one spot with a rag, and make a circular motion. The boy didn't understand the ridiculously simple motions, but in the end that preparation led to a victory when it was time to compete. The motion he had learned was the one motion he needed during the fight, and he knew it so well he could do it on autopilot, instinctively, without thinking. This is a type of physical and mental training that elite athletes use.

Consider this book a living tool that's preparing you for battle. You're going to overcome any limiting beliefs, and by the end of the process, live in full on happiness and victory!

So having said that, if you want what you want, you have to make a commitment to:

Do the assignments

Do the assignments

And most important… DO THE ASSIGNMENTS!

Transformation Leads to Multiplication

This process is designed for anyone and everyone who has a desire to make a difference in their behavior and emotions. Once you transform, you'll witness areas of your life—your joy, health, wealth, success, and mentorship abilities—multiply.

These steps will make a difference in your life, yes, but also in the lives of the people around you. When I bounced back and had my own personal transformation that night following the motorcycle accident that almost claimed my life, I knew somehow, deep inside, that I was meant to give back to others. But none of that would have been possible if I hadn't made a decision to change, because you can't give what you don't have.

Sometimes you have to take things into your own hands, so let's throw a leash on this puppy and take it for a walk.

As you develop the beliefs, behaviors, and actions that better serve who you want to become, you will impact those around you. Some will model you consciously and others will follow unconsciously. This is the power of mentorship. Pay it forward in a domino effect that changes lives.

Steps for Getting the Best

I'm assuming that if you have read this far you are about getting something new for your life and a definite result from your efforts. I'm also assuming that you are at least willing to put forth some effort to make this happen. So before we get started there are four agreements you'll need to commit to in order to get the absolute best out of this.

Agreement #1: Have Fun! You'll Learn More and Do More

Think about all the things you learned as a child.

Each time you learned something new it was an amazing phenomenon. Your senses were engaged to the fullest. Our nervous systems are set up to receive more and retain more information through our five senses. When we are alert and in a joyful and fun state of mind our senses are active and receptive. And we retain more of what we learn.

Go to www.YouTube.com and type in "child genius" and you'll find kids who excel, play piano, and do other things at the highest level. They make it playful. They even make it seem easy and effortless.

I studied "Super Learning" several years ago and one of the points that were made regarding why they can teach these young children so much so fast is the fact that children are natural fun seekers and have easier, quicker access to having fun. You see, when we are having fun and laughing, all five of our senses are more open to input, and what goes in is linked to the pleasure sensation and therefore retained and assimilated as favorable references. What that ultimately means is that when we learn things in a pleasure state it goes deeper into our nervous system and more easily and likely becomes a part of who we are.

Agreement #2: Engage, Interact and Play Full Out

No doubt you have heard before that knowledge is power. But that's a myth, because knowing something doesn't automatically make things happen. Knowledge is only potential power. In order to get it into your nervous system where it will really take hold and stick you must engage your entire self. (Don't worry, I'm going to make it so simple for you that you won't even notice that you are doing it.) You must interact and do it like it means something special, because it does. It is then that your logic, reason, emotion and psychology have no other choice but to take it in as being real and important.

Get outside your comfort zone!

Step and stay outside of your comfort zone. When we engage ourselves fully and do the things that are sometimes uncomfortable we grow in our skill and our intelligence. As long as you are going to do this you might as well do it full out, even if it feels uncomfortable. This is the time to dig in and realize that success is right around the corner. Play like you are going to win. Leave everything on the dance floor. As long as you are going to do this (spending the time, the energy, and the effort), you might as well play (and I do mean *play*) full out. If you need to do something that is outrageous, by all means do it. Play big and play to win!

Agreement #3: Have an Open Mind

Are you committed to change? That night when I was in the desert after the motorcycle crash, I had a turning point that led to transformation. Then, in the weeks that followed, I began doing things differently. I made massive immediate changes. Personal change involves adapting a new set of beliefs about what is possible.

Agreement #4: Be Consistent and Do the Exercises

This process is designed to build upon itself. Each day that you do the processes you will be strengthening your ability to be more of what you want. You will have some very simple things to do each day for approximately ten days. Make sure that you schedule the time to do them and do not miss any step.

You will be amazed at the results you get when you are consistent. Step by step I will show you how to make positive changes and how these changes will have a cumulative effect—the more you do, the better you'll get.

Let's go!

Chapter 3

THE ANATOMY OF HAPPINESS

"You are God's artist, life is the canvas and your imagination is your paint. So dip your brush in your desire and create a Masterpiece. Even if you make a mess... turn it upside down and still call it art."
—Joseph McClendon III, Ph.D.

» **CHOOSE TO CHANGE**

» **DEBUNK MYTHS**

» **ELIMINATE THINGS YOU HAVE NO USE FOR**

» **MAKE A LIST OF THINGS THAT MAKE YOU HAPPY**

When I was in my lowest state in life, I would see other guys my age driving nice cars, passing me on the street. I remember seeing one well-dressed young man in a brown suit getting out of a really nice car with shiny rims. He walked with a sense of purpose and confidence. He was going somewhere, and you know what? He didn't stop to look back.

I would see successful guys my age who seemed to have everything I didn't have and think, *I'm just as smart as he is. I should be driving that car and wearing that suit!*

Well, I've since learned that there's a huge gap between knowing something and doing it. It doesn't matter what you know. It matters what you do that creates change. I recognized that I needed to change to achieve any kind of success, but it wasn't until I had a crisis and almost got myself killed that the light bulb clicked on. In fact, even though I knew I needed to change, it didn't happen until the man in the repair shop gave me the book to read, until *I actually chose to change.*

Maybe I was a slow learner. But you've got the benefit of this book right here, right now, and you don't have to experience a crisis like I did. You can choose to change, today. Even if there's something that just doesn't feel right about your life, you can choose to make one small change in that particular area that will affect all others.

When I set out to write this book, I'd already had years of experience working with audiences and individuals across the globe on transforming thought to create a more powerful, joyful life.

But there were still new discoveries to be made. I found that there were myths I'd bought into unknowingly, which I had to discard. So here I was, an expert on the psychology of change and the science of happiness, learning something new! It's a great reminder that life is about learning. Whether you're 20 or 80, there's always something new to learn. But you have to be willing to listen, and open to receiving new information. That part is fairly easy. The important next step after that is to *choose happiness.*

Choosing to change is more than just realizing you need to change. Think about it. There are people you know today, maybe a friend, or a family member, who are stuck in some sort of negative behavior and know they need to change. Maybe it's a friend who is stuck in the victim mindset. Or perhaps it's a coworker who stays in an abusive or toxic relationship. The solution seems easy for you to see, but you're on the outside looking in. Their solution is on the inside.

Whether it is to be a happier person, stopping a bad habit, or starting a new and better behavior, all change has a structure and a specific order that makes it possible. Just like climbing in your car and turning the ignition key; there are a series of things that have to happen for the engine to start so you can drive off. There are a series of thing that have to happen within your mind and body to produce even the smallest change. And that's the anatomy of change.

We are going to be discovering those sequences of things that happen and then utilizing that structure to create the desired change called *living happy*.

Everyone Wants to Be Happy

They seek it, buy it, chase it, medicate it, and do everything possible to get it.

When we don't learn (the right way) how to be happy, we continue to chase things that we assume will make us happy. Think about the vast amount of "things" that people around you have. Apple is the world's most valuable company, hovering somewhere around $337 billion at this printing. In America, a nation riddled with debt, long lines of buyers wait for hours outside Apple stores each time a new product is released. The iPad was the fastest-selling product of all time, and Apple sells millions of them. The iPhone 4s got over 1 million pre-orders. We're not talking about a necessity here. It's not bread, milk, oxygen, or even Oreos that people are flocking to. The iPod is a device that plays music and displays photos! It's a device that makes people happy. In an economy of national debt, foreclosures, and addiction to antidepressants, what would drive people to spend much needed income so freely on toys?

There's a simple answer. People want to be happy, and they buy products that make them happy. No one needs an iPad to survive. But happiness is a powerful force, and it's not about survival. People want whatever they believe will make them happy and they're consuming more, doing more, traveling more, experiencing more, and owning more, yet there's more depression, medication, addiction, and suicide in the world than ever. All this consuming, chasing, and obtaining, yet people still aren't happy?

My five year old son can be very vocal about what he wants. But like most kids, once he gets it, it's not long before he wants something else. Sometimes he gets a fascinating new toy, and then I'm amazed at how quickly he gets bored with it. Little boys can play with a new toy car or transformer robot for 24 hours straight! Their little hands push it around the floor with joy. But in a few days, the shiny new toy sits under the bed or behind the sofa in the living room, discarded.

It's Time to Debunk the Myths about What Brings You Joy

Most people believe more money will make them happier. And it might, for a short time. But happiness must originate intrinsically, or else it will wear off pretty fast. Because for every "thing" there is an opposite, and if your belief system tells you that more money makes you happy, your belief system also tells you that less money makes you unhappy, therefore what happens when you have less? Your happiness tank feels empty.

What if you could reframe the way you think about happiness?

When I was interviewed for *O Magazine*, Oprah Winfrey's signature print periodical, I was asked about goals and specifically how people set resolutions. I answered that it's not really the *how* that matters. It's the *why*.

Most people are obsessed with the *how*—the workout routine, the foods to eat or cut out, the time it's going to take to exercise. *Why* is a much more powerful motivator. A *why* is your driver. It's the reason you want what you want and do what you do. For example, a *why* might be, *I want to be a role model for my children*, or *I want to have more energy to work and pursue my dreams, to feel good within my body.* People accomplish more by answering the question "Why am I doing this?" than "How am I doing this?" Truth is, if you have a good reason why, the *how* will follow.

So I always ask people, "What's your *why*?"

I've spoken in more than 50 countries around the world, which means I've been able to ask this question of all kinds of people in various cultures. I've met happy people, and I've encountered the opposite. I've seen people with every reason to be happy who are not, and I've met people with every conceivable reason to be miserable who are happy and content!

Ultimately I've discovered that:

» Happiness can be learned
» Happiness speeds up success
» Happiness will increase your energy
» Happiness will increase your longevity
» Happiness attracts you to what you want and what you want to you
» Happiness increases your health and wellness
» Happiness is contagious
» You can condition yourself to be habitually happy

When I reflect on my former life, which seems like someone else's life (or a movie I once saw at the theater), I remember the moment I stood in the rain at midnight and had an epiphany about life. *When things are about to change, you can feel it.* Change was in the air, and I could sense it. It was the first step on the path to happiness.

So What Is This Thing Called Happiness, Anyway?

The dictionary defines it this way:

> **Happiness** is a mental state of well-being characterized by positive emotions ranging

from a feeling or showing pleasure or contentment.

Happiness varies for everyone and it's possible that your definition up until this point has been different than mine. I've asked friends what makes them happy and the answers are all different. One says happiness is security and a healthy bank account. The other defines happiness as her kids all gathering around the same table for dinner. Another friend says he's happiest when he's on an adventure, exploring the world. But ultimately, all of those things, as varied as they are, result in the same thing: *positive emotion.*

So let's get on the same page so we have a point to start from. I like to boil it down to two simple definitions of happiness. One is a little technical and the other is what I call the lowest common denominator. Both are simple and duplicatable. Chose which one works best for you.

Happiness Definition 1:
Happiness is a mental and emotional state of being where your internal focus is optimistic, and the body produces positive energy!

or

Happiness Definition 2:
Happiness is... the feeling of joy and excitement that you get when you imagine the best and move with positive expectation.

Now that we have a point of reference to start from, wouldn't you agree that these definitions of happiness are much simpler than we've made things out to be? Happiness isn't complex, confusing, distorted, a 12-step plan, or years of agony in counseling with some self-help guru. Happiness is the feeling of joy and excitement you get when you have hope, and move with positive expectation toward that positive dream, expectation, or goal!

Happiness is just an emotion.

The beauty of that is that emotions are manufactured, and because they are manufactured they can be created and placed wherever you want them to be.

I attended the positive psychology symposium in Philadelphia, where the main focus was the effects of happiness on our lives with regard to our health, achievement, and well-being. It was brilliant. There were Ph.D.s, professors, and academics from almost every higher learning institution in the United States and abroad. The level of research and clinical study was amazing, but even though there was so much information about happiness, there weren't many solutions on how to get happy. In all the breakout sessions, discussions, and presentations, only one person asked, *"What is happiness?"*

Another thing I found odd was that the presenters didn't express happiness from within. My colleagues from *SUCCESS* magazine commented several times about the lack of smiles from the speakers and the crowd. Can you imagine that? A happiness conference where it's hard to find happy people? This is not how life is meant to be. Life is meant to be lived with full-on, explosive abundance and joy. If you're living anything less, now is the time to make a change.

The Science behind Happiness

Every emotion carries with it a certain amount of energy. Think of it as electricity because it really is. We are electrical beings and we generate electricity all day long. Let's call it *human energy*. Human energy is the state of being that perpetually produces wellness, optimism, and hope. Happy people create positive energy! And they live longer, which is a fact supported by studies of centenarians across the world. People who live beyond 100 tend to have vibrant lives, hobbies, and a happy outlook on life. They are connected to others. The science behind happiness is powerful, when you examine how a positive mindset can affect the number of years you have on this earth.

There's an important link between your body and mind when it comes to happiness. Toxic emotions create stress, impacting overall wellness. Unhappy people create negative energy. Unhappy people dwell on stress and anxiety and problems, which creates long-term health issues like heart attack, high blood pressure, stroke, or alcoholism and obesity.

Sometimes people modify their body chemistry with drugs, alcohol, or other chemicals in an attempt to get happy. Maybe you know someone who solves stress that way, or maybe that's been you. The scientific truth is that there are a multitude of happiness chemicals floating around in your brain each day. Some result in a feeling of euphoria, while others can create feelings of depression. The human body manufactures chemicals that mimic the way prescription drugs like morphine, or valium, affect your mood.

Manufacturing Joy

Drugs like morphine are powerful pain medications. Other drugs are calming, antidepressant, and send a warmth throughout the body, generating feelings of happiness. Your brain has naturally occurring chemicals that do the same thing, modulating your energy, emotions, and ability to interact with others. A chemical called dopamine operates within your body to regulate pleasure. When stress interferes with your dopamine function, your ability to enjoy life is reduced and activities you once liked no longer bring you happiness. With severe dopamine/endorphin malfunction, life becomes difficult and depressing. Days can seem dark and hopeless. People become inactive when they're depressed and don't have anything to look forward to.

How does reading that make you feel? Just thinking about depression can make you feel depressed! But the opposite is also true.

Creating Happiness

Think about the happiest moment in your life! Think about the smile of a child you love, or the time you traveled to a fantastic vacation destination and sat on a beach, or overlooked a mountain! See, aren't you already calmer and happier? A positive thought can change the way you feel. Just now, you've created happiness. Just by harnessing the power of positive thought. You didn't have to examine your bucket list, adventure to the Andes, sign up for a yearlong project to become happy or set ridiculous goals. You didn't have to climb Mount Kilimanjaro. All you had to do is think about the happy moments and people in your life. Thinking happy thoughts generates the biological response that leads to joy, calm, and peace within your soul.

Endorphins, those natural chemicals that you get from various things like exercise, sex, and sometimes even chocolate, give you a natural feeling of temporary euphoria. Did you realize that there are literally thousands of chemical reactions going on inside you each day? Natural occurring morphine-like molecules are made in your brain. Is it any wonder humans face a myriad of emotional swings?

There have been a lot of books written on happiness. Some encourage you to try different adventures every month for a year until you're happy. But you could do that and end up chasing the wind. You could read a book on happiness or participate in a project about happiness and end up really unhappy a year after you put the book down. That's because happiness is an emotion, yes, but there are physical realities that create and drive your emotions. There are scientific components, chemicals, and processes at work within your brain and body that generate feelings, and chemicals that make you happy (or sad.)

The truth is: *You are not stuck with the state you're in now. If you're unhappy, you don't have to be.*

Debunking Myths and Obstacles to Happiness

One day I was pulling out of my driveway on my Harley-Davidson motorcycle and my five-year-old son and his little friend opened the door and let my dog out, unbeknownst to me. Now Winston is a French bulldog, and he's the cutest thing in the world, but he is dumber than a box of wood. My crazy dog goes nuts when he sees the motorcycle. He just goes mad trying to bite the tires as though the bike is an evil beast trying to harm his family. It's a weird quirk the dog has, but we all have quirks, don't we?

Well on that particular day I didn't know that Winston had gotten out and I roared off on my bike so fast that I didn't even see him chasing me! He must have been in my blind spot. I went about my business and in about an hour or so I returned to find that I had flattened my dog Winston. I had run over him by accident.

My wife was left behind with the wreckage of the poor dog and she had rushed him to the vet and was just pulling into the driveway as I returned. At first I was mortified and I felt terrible. Not just because I flattened Winston but because my son and his little buddy saw the whole thing. The good news is that even though the dog was all beat up and cut up and had tire marks from head to foot, he survived! He had no internal damage or broken bones, and even funnier, the boys were giggling their butts off because they watched Winston get run over and then get up and continue to chase the bike until he ran out of steam. They thought it was hilarious. My son even got a couple of his toys and reenacted the event.

But here's the interesting thing. Even though ol' Winston was all beat up and cut up and even though he was in a drugged-up stupor from the medication that the vet gave him, as soon as he saw the bike again he went right back into full-on attack mode. He literally would have done it again, and was blind to the fact that he almost got his ass killed. He's fine today, but that was one blind spot that could've been fatal!

It's a good reminder to always be on the lookout for the blind spots in your life and systematically seek and destroy them. Replace them with mirrors and windows so that you can see clearly where you want to go.

Do You Have a Blind Spot?

Before you can change the way you think you have to examine yourself and be open to the possibility that you might have blind spots. You may not know what lies you've believed until someone or something causes you to think a different way. We all have blind spots. Some are minor, but others are fatal! The good news is that if you can dig deep enough to discover your blind spots, or wrong ways of thinking, you can turn things around.

Life Can Be Just As Exciting at 70 As It Was at 19

In my case, life is overwhelmingly happier now than it was when I was 19! But I had to make the changes necessary to get here. When I started working on this book I wanted to create something that had never been done before. I wasn't having any kind of midlife crisis, and I wasn't lacking anything in particular except for a desire to see others change, rapidly! I knew that a book could be a multiplying force in changing lives. Instead of just delivering a few hundred pages of random information, I decided to compress decades of what I'd learned, and seen work in others, to build a living tool. So this isn't just a book, but a tool that will help you create your own personal happiness action plan!

It doesn't matter if you want to make one major change, or several small ones. Change is growth. You can eliminate just one habit, and your entire world could transform. Change is like a wave in the ocean. One small one can create a ripple effect that leads to a tsunami of events. To prove this let's use a familiar example of a minor change with magnificent results. Let's say you have a nagging habit of losing your keys. It's always irritating, especially on days when you need to get somewhere fast. Irritation turns to anger, and then stress, when the event you've got to get to is an important work interview, or a life-changing obligation. Imagine how the stress level would increase if you had to get to a court-appointed date, at a specific time, yet couldn't find your keys! If you miss the appointment, you've got potential fines and legal problems. All of a sudden, any interruption from a family member turns into an explosion. You snap off a curt, angry remark. You say things you don't mean, and accuse others of taking your keys. Suddenly a bad habit of misplacing your keys snowballs into a bigger problem: relational turmoil.

One simple yet positive change would be to get a basket for your keys and place it in the kitchen, or to hang a hook on the wall. Instantly, a potential stressor is removed from your life and household. When we remove stress, we increase happiness! That's the concept of eliminating what you have no use for. You have absolutely no use for time wasters that detract from your life and create stress. When you eliminate them, you instantly increase your happiness bank account.

Choose to change. Start now by making a list of three things that waste your time that you'd like to eliminate from your day, week, and life. When most people think about this simple concept of eliminating things they have no use for, it's life-changing. One simple exercise. Eliminate what you have no use for, and create more space for happiness to enter. Believe it or not, just writing them down will produce less stress. Try it…. You'll like it.

Things to eliminate that waste my time:

1. _____

_____

2. _____

_____

3. _____

_____

4. _____

_____

5. _____

_____

Remember, our goal is to produce more happiness, and a big part of doing that is to program ourselves to think differently. I had to learn to think differently in order to live differently. And you can too. *Carpe diem!* Now is the time to start having fun on your journey. Let's roll.

THE TRUTH ABOUT CHANGE

"A lie gets halfway around the world before the truth has a chance to get its pants on."
—*Winston Churchill*

» **ADOPT A WARRIOR MENTALITY**

» **BE COACHABLE**

» **BE COMMITTED TO CHANGE**

Inside of you is a warrior ready to conquer the world!

You were wired for happiness, adventure, and abundance. Those attributes were embedded into your soul from birth, from the moment you burst forth out of the womb. You didn't enter this world with a whimper. You entered it bold and defiant!

But along the way you might have been unconsciously rewired. Your great and empowering experiences, relationships, discoveries, triumphs, breakthroughs, and celebrations may have impacted the way that you think about what is possible in your life. Your bad experiences, relationships, struggles, defeats, tragedies, encounters with bullies or classmates, and even work obstacles, may have impacted the way you think about what's not possible in your life. You may have lowered your expectations! You may have bought into lies that ultimate, extreme, full-on happiness just isn't possible.

Look Back but Don't Stare

When I write or speak about my past it feels unnatural, because I'm not the kind of guy to dwell on the past. Our lives are full of peaks and valleys and sometimes it's important to use your life experience to teach others about what's possible, but if you're always looking back, you can't see the road ahead. If you're driving your car down the highway intent on getting to a certain destination, it is physically impossible to look backward and drive forward. Eventually you're going to crash.

> **THE CHANGE WE ARE TALKING ABOUT ISN'T GENERIC. IT'S CHANGE TO LIVE HAPPY.**

When people are depressed and at their lowest, they feel locked up in the pain of their own perception of how bad things are. They dwell on the mistakes they have made and how others have done them wrong. The pain and confusion gets multiplied because they keep looking at what has happened and reliving it even if it is not true. They feel locked up and emotionally drained because they are not looking forward with positive expectation.

People who attach the bad from the past to the present project it into the future. So now they are unhappy about the past, the present, and the future!

In this book you will learn to look forward to each day with positive expectation and how to manufacture your own happiness, in order to be the person you were destined to be. I wasn't created to be broke, busted, and disgusted, and neither were you! I wasn't created to be depressed, and you weren't either! Remember, happiness is just an emotion. And all emotions are manufactured, and therefore can be deconstructed and made anew.

Be Who You Were Destined to Be

In these pages, I'm honored to be your coach. This book is a living tool that, if used properly, will guide you to the attitude (and therefore life) of your dreams. You will perceive the world a different way. Your subconscious reactions will change. Your nervous system will manufacture happiness until you wake up each day wanting to set the world on fire! And in order for all that to happen you've got to be coachable and willing to receive.

When my son was about four years old I had the opportunity to teach him the importance of coaching and the anatomy of listening and I could instantly see the light bulb click on in his brain. He got it! He's the happiest kid I know. Really, I know most parents will gush about their kids but my son is so happy and joyful that he's always smiling, and even if he gets upset about something he's just a heartbeat from busting out in full-on giggles. But we've worked to help create and install happiness in his life and in his way of thinking. Imagine if you could learn this process and pass it on to a younger generation! Instead of the old method of laboriously long psychology sessions many adults sit through to relive old traumas and tragedies year after year, imagine if you could compress overcoming adversity and teach a new way of embracing and installing happiness and feelings of joy into the nervous system. Together, we could change the world!

My son sat down at the computer with me one day as I taught him about the power of being coachable and learning new things. I said; "Throughout your life you will need a coach. In order to get anywhere, fast, it's important to use a coach." I pulled up a boxing match on YouTube and showed him a brief clip. The professional boxers fought a round, and then the bell rang and they retreated to their corners. In the corners their coaches talked to them, and the boxers nodded and went right back out for another round. I stopped the video. "What just happened?" I asked.

My son reported what he saw. "The boxers sat down and a man came over and talked to them."

I hit play once again, and the same process was repeated. The boxers fought a good round, the bell rang, and each one went back to their corners. In the corner their coaches gave them advice. I stopped it and told my son; "See how the boxer didn't argue with his coach and didn't ask questions. He just learned what he needed to know to go back out there and win the fight." I told him that the fastest way to win the fight is to listen to the coach.

But most people want to do it alone! (This is why most people give up on their dreams when they don't achieve them.)

Be Coachable

I've always been interested in the mind and what makes us tick. When I was in college toward the end of one of my lengthy psychology courses I remember feeling extremely discouraged. As a matter of fact I was so discouraged that I made the decision that the line of work was not for me. We had a guest speaker in on that day and her topic was "The Business of Psychology" and after about a half hour of semi-boring facts and figures she opened herself up for questions. One of the other students asked, "How much income can we expect to make per year? What's the maximum pay and how long will it take us to get there?"

Without skipping a beat and with a bit of a smirk on her face the speaker replied, "Psychology is the only profession that you get paid for not being successful."

This brought about a mixture of uncomfortable laughter and exasperation from the class. She stood there with a look that clearly said she was proud of herself but not sure if she should be! You could tell that this wasn't the first time that she used that line, but she was probably used to getting a much more favorable response. We all sat there in uncomfortable silence until I couldn't take it. I wanted to know what she meant, so I raised my hand and asked her to explain.

"If you have a problem," she said, "and I fix it in one or two visits, you won't be coming back every week to give me a hundred dollars."

I was mortified!

"Why would you let someone suffer if you could do something about it?" I asked.

She chuckled. "Of course I'm being a bit facetious but there is some truth to it, isn't there? These things take time and we are being paid by the hour. It could take months even years to help someone."

I wanted no part of something that was going to have that type of mentality around it so I swore off pursuing that career. In reality I wasn't really that interested in becoming a psychologist for a living and that was just the excuse I needed to divert all of my attention to my true passion at the moment, which was playing music and becoming a recording artist to secure a deal with a record company. So off I went.

Five years later I was introduced to the neurosciences. I studied neurolinguistic programming, neuro-associative conditioning, hypnotherapy, and the brain. It changed my life and my opinion about helping people this way. I learned how to do in hours and days what used to take months and years, and I became certified and opened a practice in Los Angeles.

In the last chapter I talked about eliminating the things that don't work for you anymore. Sometimes you have to let go of things to have the life you were destined for. When I let go of the path I was on, I was able to step into a profession where I began changing lives immediately.

I began working from sunup to sundown. I put an ad in

the local paper that said, "If you have a fear or a phobia or any emotional challenge call me and I'll handle it right now." My phone rang off the hook and I had more business than I had time. It was Los Angeles, near Hollywood, so the freaks came out of the woodwork. I met one woman who was deathly afraid of her own fingernails. She had worn gloves since she was a little girl, only taking them off to wash her hands and change gloves. It was an amazing time because the variety of people caused me to learn more and sharpen my game. I got really good really fast. In most cases I could produce major change in just one visit and the people would refer others to me because they were so happy.

Along the way I adopted a system that works for compressing results. Since then, I've discovered that most people are truly satisfied when they're operating in their passion, destiny, and full potential. You can't be as happy as you should be if you feel like something's missing.

How Happy Can You Really Be?

When you are living in the fullness of life, you begin to see that you have no limitations. Although I'm not a medical doctor, I do hold a doctorate in neuropsychology and one of my passions and gifts is in the area of health and wellness. I juice, eat specific foods, and for decades generally have studied physiology and how the body works. People often tell me I look several years younger than my real age. I wrote a book called *Change Your Breakfast, Change Your Life*, and it's successful because I delivered material I was passionate about and gifted to share.

I share this with you because there is no separation between the mind and the body. What is happening with the physical body is also happening with your brain. Your brain is physical and organic in nature and works in conjunction with literally every other part of your body. They are all interconnected and what happens to one will affect all of the others on some level. Understanding this one simple fact will change how you look at attaining and sustaining happiness, or any emotion, for that matter. In my opinion this is also the most overlooked area in the field of psychology and possibly the most important. Although it helps to be healthy, I'm not saying that unless you are in perfect health you can't be happy. But what you do with your body in terms of movement is one of the greatest components of the state of happiness!

When you move, you gain momentum.

Physical movement or lack thereof is one-third of any emotion. You'll learn more about this shortly as well as how to use the information to produce happiness and joy. Your body and brain are wired for happiness. Countless laboratory experiments and brain science studies report that positive moods reduce stress-related hormones. This chemical chain reaction increases the immune function in the human body, promoting health, healing, and vitality. When you look at the scientific data, you can see that happiness isn't an option but a necessity, as important as air and water.

Happiness makes your body strong and your brain work better. You're supposed to be happy. You were constructed for it!

Time to Get Happy!

No doubt you've had an interesting life full of relationships, friends, jobs, travel, and wins along the way. You've achieved a measure of success, but you can't help but think there's much more than what's in front of you right now. God created in you a brain wired for happiness, a body wired for movement, and a soul wired for success, not failure. But the world is set up completely opposite.

Mankind was created for adventure. But most of the world shuns it, favoring steadfastness, the security of a 9-to-5 paycheck, and responsibility. From the days of the very first explorers, man has navigated and roamed the wilds, his soul longing for newness, excitement, and discovery. Man was created with long, strong arms and legs, and a solid center core and he was built with questions within his soul as vast as the highest mountain. Who am I? Is there more out there? What was my heart created for? Questions that can't be resolved by sitting behind a computer screen. Yet years have gone by and here we are, unnaturally tethered to the manmade box, answering email. Man is an explorer by nature, wired for extreme happiness! So what has kept us from it?

When you are stressed, your biological response is similar to a car that was filled with corrupted fuel. The engine would sputter at best, overheat, and if driven too long that way, self-destruct. Unhappiness creates stress hormones that negatively impact your biology and the way you think and perform.

It's important to change whatever it is that we need to change to get what you want in terms of maintaining happiness in your life. In order to do this it is imperative that you understand and believe first that change is possible. As simplistic as that may sound many people either never even think of it or, if they do, they think that they are somehow stuck with who and what they are. People tend to believe they are somehow locked into a certain way of being as a result of our having been born into a certain socioeconomic level. Or that due to the physical structure of our bodies and the looks that come along with it we are destined to be, do, and have a certain type of life. This is the type of thinking that prevails in countries that have a caste society. Where you were born determines where and how you will live your life. Royalty is royalty and common is common.

So for the sake of going further faster let's adopt the philosophy that no one is stuck with who they are and that everyone can change. As a matter of fact everyone will change just by virtue of the fact that we all must adapt to the changing world around us. The question is, How much will they change, how quickly, and will they be more or less happy along the journey?

There are two types of change: involuntary and voluntary. Passive (involuntary) change is where we adapt to our surroundings habitually and unconsciously. Voluntary change is deliberate and even though we might not like what we have to do we take the initiative and systematically, consciously, make a change in behavior and thought.

Change from the Inside Out

By far the majority of change in most people's lives is involuntary or unintentional. We are adaptive creatures and the fast pace of life dictates that we must change unconsciously just to be able to keep up. This along with the fact that we are constantly being bombarded with message after message from every conceivable form of media to adjust our way of life to fit in and thrive makes it almost impossible to keep track of what is happening from the inside out. I operate from one simple belief with regard to producing human magnificence: If someone can achieve something then so can I (and so can anyone else) and we can do it faster and better if we want to.

You have changed and you continue to change. If you have any doubt about that consider this. You used to poop your pants. That's right, at one point in your life you felt completely comfortable with dropping a load right there in your diaper. You didn't think anything of it and it seemed like that was the right thing to do. Then at some point you learned that you needed to make a change and you did. For most of us it was a progressive change, but it did occur. At other points in our lives, change occurs in the blink of an eye.

What Is True Change?

There are many different forms of change and many different definitions for change so for the sake of us all being on the same page consider this: Change is simply the transformation of one form into another. Isn't that simple? Whether it's changing your mind, changing behavior, or even a change in the weather.

Whatever form it was in one minute it changes to another form the next. There is gradual change and there is sudden change and all stages in between. There is incremental change and there is exponential or geometric change. Incremental change is slow and timely. Geometric change is faster and multiplies quickly. Think of geometric change as compounded interest. At first it seems small and insignificant but once it starts to multiply it grows like crazy. This is what we are going to be doing with our happiness.

Change is possible. You have changed, you will change, and more change is inevitable.

Google any success story and you will be inundated with web pages of men and women who were in completely undesirable situations who shifted their way of thinking and behaving to create something else. They changed how they think, how they talked, how they moved, and what they believed to adapt their behaviors to the needs of their desired outcomes. And though every journey is different, the process of change was exactly the same. I call this process the anatomy of change. Understanding it will allow us to model the process and compress time.

Chapter 5

CONSTRUCTING HAPPINESS

- » **CHANGE THE THING THAT WILL MAKE THE BIGGEST DIFFERENCE**

- » **KNOW YOUR DESTINATION**

- » **FIND WHAT HOLDS YOU BACK**

- » **OBLITERATE IT TO CREATE SPACE**

- » **FILL THE SCOTOMA (SPACE) WITH POSITIVE BEHAVIORS AND EMOTIONS**

Life is a great journey filled with victories, battles, and mountains to climb along the way. If you plan to achieve any amount of success, you're going to face obstacles. Speed bumps are everywhere you go. Stop viewing them as deterrents to slow you down and start looking at them as brief pauses on the road of life. A speed bump, an obstacle, or even a deep hole or tragedy is just a moment in time. It's a part of life that will pass.

How we respond, and how we pick ourselves back up and start again, is what matters.

Today is a new day, and you are a warrior! Put on your armor, shield, and breastplate and pick up your sword. There is a time for everything, a season for every single thing under the sun. Dance when you need to and grieve when you need to. But then remember to pick up your sword and get right back on the battlefield again because the victory and rewards are yours! I use this metaphor of the battle because life isn't always easy. It would be unfair to present it that way.

And although this process is simple, there is a bit of a battle that needs to take place.

The battle is between the old way of thinking and the new way of thinking and behaving. This book is a lifting tool, and the truth is, in order to win and overcome and get what you want, sometimes it's a fight! At times you'll have to slay dragons that you've grown accustomed to living with. Those are the things you've held onto because it seems harder to go through the process of letting them go or you simply have become comfortable with them. But battle doesn't have to be lengthy or bloody. It can be exhilarating and swift. When you adopt a warrior mindset (versus a victim mindset) you WILL be victorious. In the end, you will have redemption and victory over negative thought processes and behaviors.

People Are Resistant to Change

So many people believe they have seemingly given themselves no other choice but to drown in the quicksand of their life circumstances. It's because they see the quicksand, not the possibilities of the future.

We all know people who are terminally unhappy—victims of their upbringing, life experiences, teachers, or tragedies. These are the people who seem to be stuck in a downward pattern year after year! And the truth is, they just don't know the truth. They don't realize that it's possible to be happy despite life circumstances as long as they're willing to transform. But that's not you. You picked up this book, and you're ready. So even if you're surrounded by naysayers, or live with one of those people resistant to change, vow to engage in your own success and happiness today. Don't look back, don't look sideways, don't examine or criticize them. When you do that, it's a distraction to your full-on, abundant life, and everyone has a different path. Their timing may not be the same as yours. Look forward. It's your life, and this is your moment.

Know Your Destination

The question right now is, *What will you decide to change?* And the best answer to that question is to make the decision to change the things that will make the biggest difference. Change the one thing that will have a profound impact on all of the other areas of your life.

Think about it for a minute, and write it down here.

I will change:

_____

_____

_____

_____

_____

_____

_____

Your level of happiness will multiply in a domino effect. So the smartest thing to key in on to make substantial change is the change in your personal happiness.

So How Do Humans Change?

The anatomy of change starts with the structure and the strategy, just like building a car or constructing a house. There is a predictable, duplicatable process. Homebuilders pour the concrete slab, frame the house, and then build interior rooms, put on the roof, spackle, paint, and finish out. There are a lot more steps to the process of building a house, including preparation and architecture, but the process is duplicatable and all homebuilders go through similar steps regardless of how unique they are as craftsman and their commitment to quality. It could be said that a house is just a house, and that's a great analogy because a human is just a human. But as we talk through change and transformation, you can also say that not all houses or humans are the same. I've walked into homes that knock your socks off because you can see clearly how the homeowner was committed to magnificence. One friend of mine bought a home and renovated it, until the walls literally popped with color, the ceilings sparkled with chandeliers and lustrous lighting, and the dingy old floors were shined up to a fabulous new glossy surface. The rooms of the house had once been vacant, yet now overflowed with warmth and vibrancy. The house started as basic foundation, bricks, and mortar, and ended up fantastic after an internal and external transformation.

The following are the steps in the human change process. Each step relies on the previous to create the foundation for impacting the nervous system and producing growth. So don't skip a step! It's like renovating that house, or training to win the Tour de France. I'm pretty sure you can't just show up and win. First, you need a bike. And it has to be the right bike. Next, you need a good solid training program, endurance, practice, the right foods, a strong practice and training regimen before the race, and a winning mindset. Skip any of those and it's unlikely you'll win.

The 5-Step Process to Human Change

When it comes to this process of change, the new emotional and behavioral patterns will become automatic and habitual. There is a strategy to change that just works. It works because it draws on the natural way your body operates. The steps are the same steps that everyone goes through when they make change, whether they know it or not. They are the same steps that I went through laying in the mud screaming "I'm a man" and declaring it was going to change now. And these are the same steps I use to create change with my clients and students.

The five steps to human behavioral and emotional change are:

1) Destination
2) Hesitation
3) Obliteration
4) Creation
5) Automation

I will be going into each of them in much more detail and how to simply use them when we get into the actual process. But for now here is a short explanation of each of them.

Step 1: Destination (Navigation)

In order to get where we are going we must first know where we are and where we want to go. Without a target we don't know where to aim. With a target and a destination we can put our internal GPS to work to bring it to us and us to it. Also, the more specific we are about where we want to go the better we are able to get there faster. Knowing that our destination is happiness is great and each individual has their own particular internal interpretation of what that is. So it is important that we find your personal happiness destination. Doing this one thing is the most important part of the whole process and the one that most guess at if they even do it at all. Once we have the destination we must find the best path to get there. Navigation is mapping out and planning how to go from Point A to Point B. But first you must understand where you are now! It's like using MapQuest to get where you want to go in a new city versus just guessing.

In this case Point B is the destination called individual, consistent happiness and Point A is the consistent emotional state that one currently experiences in their day-to-day lives. Once you have these two points you can successfully create a path to follow. Most people are in complete denial as to where they really are in relation to where they want to be.

A key emotional component of step one is justification. When we find the reasons why we want what we want we will justify our change in behavior. We will rationalize with ourselves and come up with reasons for going through the discomfort associated with change. Interestingly enough we use this same process to stay the same and continue to do the things that don't serve us. We instinctively justify the reasons to stay the same.

Human beings will do more for their reasons than they will ever do for their outcomes. Our entire motivation comes from the reasons why we want or don't want something. This force is so great that we will justify any behavior to support it. I call it your pulling force. It pulls you away from things, feelings, and behaviors and toward others.

Once we find out what these points of pull are we can use them to leverage change.

Step 2: Hesitation

What is it that causes people to hesitate at the gates of freedom? The answers are as varied as the stars on a hot summer night. And all of them come with a reason why. Now is the time to uncover it and eliminate it.

For every procrastination there is an equal or greater hesitation. There is always a reason why someone does what they do. Something is triggering them to behave that way. What stops you from feeling the way you want is important to discover, so that we can deal with it accordingly.

This step is about finding the gremlin first before we can kill it because gremlins multiply.

Finding that thing that holds you back will give you the intelligence you need to gear up for the final showdown. Once you find it you can flush it out and see it for what it really is. This step is not to be confused with the originating factor or factors that caused the challenge in the first place. Just like in finding the reasons when we want what we want will pull us into doing more. The same mechanism has been in play for why we haven't made the change in the past. Finding out how we justify the bad behaviors and feelings will give us valuable leverage to create change. It will knock the wind out of the sails of procrastination and hesitation.

Step 3: Obliteration

In my opinion the biggest reason why people don't change is because they don't do anything about their existing pattern of behavior and emotion. They try to add on something new without making room for it.

In the practice of neurolinguistic programming this process is called interrupting the pattern. Whenever a person is in a particular pattern of thought, behavior, or emotion, if that pattern is interrupted, that interruption will cause a blank spot in the mind. The blank spot interrupts everything, including emotion. This is what we are going to do in exercises throughout this book.

A blank spot is called a *scotoma*. Derived from the Greek word for darkness, a scotoma in ophthalmology is simply a blind spot in the visual field. Medically, it's a small impairment of visual acuity, but it doesn't enter your consciousness because it's too small. Everyone has scotomas. Psychologically, scotomas exist when our focus has been drawn to a specific thing. We tend to block out other things that are around in an effort to stay focused on our target. We also create scotomas when we act on the way we believe things to be, rather than the truth. Sometimes we can't see the blind spot. If you're driving, and there's a semi in your blank area and you change lanes without looking, the blind spot could be deadly.

The most useful part about scotomas is that we can deliberately create them and use them to our advantage. We've all had blank spaces occur, or blank moments where we got interrupted and couldn't remember what it was we were talking about or thinking.

Here's a simple example. You're sitting in your living room and you decide to get up and go get a glass of water. You stand up and walk into the kitchen and there you are looking around confused, trying to remember what you went in there for! When it happens, it's a weird feeling. In reality, when you stood up and moved your body you actually interrupted the pattern of thought and emotion that you were in sitting on the couch. You interrupted yourself and it caused you to draw a blank.

The other interesting thing about creating a blank spot is that blank spot acts as a vacuum in your mind. It's not just a blank hole. It's a blank space yearning to be filled with something. Nature hates a vacuum and it will take in just about anything in the moment. The beauty of this point is that you are never more susceptible to suggestion as you are when you are in a scotoma state.

The mind is a valuable tool in the war against un-resourceful patterns and behaviors. It is possible to deliberately interrupt a negative pattern and create space to be filled with something useful. Do this enough time the right way and you will destroy the original pattern of emotion and replace it with the desired emotion and subsequent behavior. It is possible to obliterate negative thoughts, emotions, and behaviors and create space for the good to flow in, and as you travel through this process with me I'll guide you to do just that.

Step 4: Creation

Remember Step 1: navigation. We determine what it is we want. But in reality everything that we want is a feeling. *An emotion.* Those feelings will precede any behavior.

Remember when you were 17 and had feelings for someone special? Maybe it was your first real relationship and your heart skipped a beat when you thought about that person. The emotions, hormones, and beliefs were amped up and linked to getting what you wanted. When we remember those things in our past that make us feel good, we can capture those feelings to be used to our advantage. And here's the real cool part. Your mind can't tell the difference between what's real and what's not when you imagine it vividly.

So we now take that destination emotion and this is where we place it into the space that we created with the obliteration process. Remember that the mind wants control and seeks answers, so if there is a vacuum it feels unnatural. When we make the space it is searching for something to fill it. And here is when we place in that spot what it is we really want.

Step 5: Automation

We not only can install those feelings in the scotoma that we create, but we can also condition our nervous system to accept them as real and they will become a part of who we are.

So instead of having to remind yourself to be happy or respond favorably, this step conditions the nervous system to accept that the desired emotion and subsequent behavior is its natural default. This is where you utilize things that naturally occur in your life to actually trigger you to be happy.

This is how our bodies, muscle memory, and the nervous system have worked for millions of years, so all we are doing is taking advantage of this process and directing it in the direction that we desire. It's not brainwashing, or guru theory. We aren't replacing your natural spirituality, destiny, or connection with God with any programming. We are adding, not subtracting. You are enhancing the foundation of who you are by replacing dysfunctional or outdated beliefs with a new program.

An Exercise for You!

Pretty cool, huh? So now that you know where you are going, let's start right away with where you are by going back to Step 1: Destination (Navigation). I'm going to keep this exercise simple for now.

Remember that in order to get where you are going you have to know where you are.

Navigation is going from Point A to Point B. But first you must understand where you are now! This exercise is designed for clarity and focus.

Take a moment to think realistically about where you are, and what you want to change. Think about the things that stress you and detract from your success. If it's paying bills late, and accruing hundreds of dollars of late fees as a result, be open and honest with yourself about why you avoid looking at bills. Procrastination is the root of it. If you have problems in business or in a relationship, write them down. The point of this exercise is to honestly understand where you are, in order to navigate out of it.

I'm successful in many areas, but the things I'd like to work to be happier overall are:

_____

_____

_____

_____

_____

_____

_____

_____

_____

_____

_____

_____

_____

_____

_____

I could be much more understanding, patient, or focused on certain things. I could increase my character traits (patience, love, giving, joy, discipline) and become better at:

Most people are in complete denial as to where they really are in relation to where they want to be. A key emotional component of Step 1 is justification. If I would've answered those questions when I was 19 and homeless, my first thoughts would have been to justify my situation subconsciously because I'd been wronged or hurt by people or because of my circumstances, or because of this or because of that. Later, when I got some sense knocked into me I would've responded more honestly. I saw the light. I was able to overcome pride, resistance, and a downward spiral of negative behaviors and stop justifying failure. There's simply no option to fail.

When we find the reasons why we want what we want we will justify our change in behavior. We will rationalize with ourselves and come up with reasons for going through the discomfort associated with change.

GETTING FOCUSED ON WHAT MATTERS MOST

Eugene O'Kelly had it all.

He was the CEO of KPMG, one of the world's top three largest accounting firms. He had a beautiful home, a family, and a stellar career. He was highly methodical and organized, accustomed to getting what he wanted. And he was a bold, anything-is-possible thinker, persistent about finding complex solutions. One time, when he wanted to talk to a banker who was particularly difficult to get in touch with, Eugene booked a seat on a long international flight next to the man just to have time to talk to him. His unique approach and persistence paid off. He got the client.

But then a routine doctor visit changed his life. The doctor found an abnormal spot on his brain, and the MRI showed three tumors, each about the size of a golf ball. It was an aggressive form of brain cancer, defined as stage 4 astrocytoma.

I've worked with CEOs, and they're

in that position for a reason. It's not just schooling or merely a degree that gets them there. They possess a certain skill set that distinguishes them from the rest. Most CEOs are strategic thinkers with the ability to asses, understand, and find solutions for their employees and organizations. Their job is to manage and lead individuals and teams to greatness. A CEO needs to think! He needs his whole brain.

Yet Eugene said: "I was blessed. I was told I had three months to live."

The CEO began to prepare for the end of his life methodically, creating an action plan that resembled a business plan. He started by making a detailed list that included what he called unwindings, the process of putting closure to his relationships, as well as planning his own funeral. For the unwinding exercise, he drew concentric circles, listing the names of his brief acquaintances in the outermost, then his business colleagues in an inner circle, and then his extended family, and then his innermost loved ones at the core.

It was the core circle people he wanted to spend the most time with, so he devised a plan to "unwind" with people in the outermost circles with a phone call, a face-to-face brief meeting, or some other closure process. He met one friend on a park bench and broke the news, always conscious of not wasting too much time drawing things out. It was a challenge, because people had a natural desire to follow up and spend more time with him once they knew he was dying. But even as they sobbed, reminisced, and asked to meet him for lunch or dinner, he had to tell them that it was the last time they'd ever see him again. Because that person was not in the inner core, he had to limit time spent with them.

And then, as if that isn't enough for a man who has been told he's got three months to live, he decided to write a book! In his final days, Eugene O'Kelly wrote *Chasing Daylight: How My Forthcoming Death Transformed My Life.*

If You Had Less Than 100 Days to Live, How Would You Spend Them?

What would you do? No one really knows how many days they have left on earth. It might be thirty, or it might be three decades. No one knows what the future holds. But whether its four months or forty years I'm sure you will agree with me that as much of that precious time should be spent as happy as possible.

If you're not working toward it, your emotions can be out of synch. Understand how to be happier and get more of what you want by understanding the link between your mind and body. And then doing something about it is key to your magnificent future. When you are happy, smiling, and creating positive energy, your body is calm and relaxed, with blood pressure at normal levels. When you're stressed, blood pressure increases and body physiology is altered.

Be Committed to the Anatomy of Change

If you're like most people, you may have had negative messages, people, and life experiences crushing your dreams. You might have believed lies, and given up on yourself or some of the things you wanted to achieve. But today is a new day. In order for real change to occur, you have to be willing to wipe the slate clean. What does that mean? It means that you have to be willing to eliminate your prior beliefs. You have to be open to the possibility that there's a better way to think.

Remember our definition of happiness?

Happiness is a mental and emotional state of being where your internal focus is optimistic, and the body produces positive energy!

Let go of your misconceptions, judgments, and preconceived notions and know that anything that is not activity is just another excuse. What if your entire future rides on how much you invest here in this process right now? Don't put it off another day. The quality of your life is the quality of your wellness. As dramatic as this may sound, it is extremely and profoundly important to view where you are right now as a pivotal point in your life.

In my speaking engagements to large audiences, I often talk about the power of laughter. I encourage people to infuse laughter into their lives. Why? Because it's healing. I saw this in my own life when my mother was diagnosed with terminal cancer. I went out and purchased funny videos and played them for her until she laughed. In the midst of tragedy, we laughed. And there was a lot of healing that came from it. I truly believe my mother's life was extended due to the power of laughter, and the positive attitude we adopted.

The Power of Laughter

As it turns out, all of those goofy little sayings and clichés that our parents used to say were grounded in solid, scientific foundation. A smile is just a frown turned upside down! And let us not forget: Laughter is the best medicine.

Your physiology is directly connected to your mind and together they produce feelings and emotions. It's safe to say that how we are moving and thinking is how we are being. Our minds and bodies are inseparable and completely connected in every way. Trying to change how we feel without including a change in some or all of our body movements is like trying to drive your car with two flat tires.

Laughter really is the best medicine.

Laughter is like medicine for the soul! Literally. Studies show that laughing itself increases joy, and makes you forget about stressors, and stressful life events and triggers. When you watch a comedian, listen to someone funny, and laugh a deep guffaw from the bottom of your diaphragm, your countenance changes. Laughter manufactures joy. And don't even get me started on the amount of energy you transmit and the level of physical attractiveness and material attractiveness you produce when you laugh. The health benefits are astronomical.

When Mom was diagnosed with terminal cancer and the physicians told my sister and me that she had two months to live, of course we were shocked. But I had previously read a book by a Dr. Norman Cousins where he had cured himself of a terminal disease and credited laughter with his remission. Mama and our family started on a regimen of laughter and joy. By also changing her diet and a few other things, she lived another eleven and a half years and was cancer free.

When laughter is authentic and uninhibited it frees up the diaphragm for deeper breathing, and triggers the release of endorphins. It brings more oxygen to the bloodstream and helps the body repair itself. When you laugh you stimulate several things in the body, not the least of which is the fact that when you laugh it forces you to take deep breaths. The increased oxygen gives cells what they need and the movement of the lymph eliminates toxins.

In supercentenerian studies (people who live to 115 or more), socialization and an outgoing personality are big factors. People who are happy live longer and have deeper relationships. People who can laugh and be lighthearted when things go wrong manage stress better.

James Smith, CEO and former NFL player, says: "I'm not always happy but I'm positive about the direction I'm going! And that makes me happy!"

Laughter and happiness cannot be underestimated.

Real, true, from-the-belly laughter is a momentary escape from the anxiety of the day. It's like a magic pill that erases any memory and floods the body instantly with happy chemicals. Also, in order for you to laugh, you have to shift your focus from something that is potentially not so good to something that is. Laughing also causes your brain to release chemicals that make you feel good, and there's a domino effect, because the more you laugh, the better you feel and healthier you get.

I experience this often in my own life. I can laugh and feel instant change in my body. It's like a magic elixir and it fills your veins with a positive energy automatically. It's the same way when you go to a concert, and listen to your favorite live music. It can be like a profound experience that changes your soul. Music invades your hearing senses but reverberates through your soul. That's one reason churches, speakers, and other major conference events use music to kick off the experience because it gets people into a completely different state, and speaks to people on a subconscious level. Music can change us, lift us, and make us feel happy emotions just through the tone, style, lyrics, or sound. It's a great way to set the stage and wipe the slate clean from the stresses of the day.

Laughter produces the same biochemical result in your body!

Later in this book I'll take you through a process to stimulate your laughter reserves and attach it to your way of being. But for now, understand that you are in control of your entire mind and body and the more you seek joy, laugh, and smile, the more you will cultivate and sustain them. The proverb that says "As ye seek so shall ye find" is only giving us half of the equation. It should continue to state that as ye seek so shall ye continue to seek and continue to find and feel." Okay, okay I made that part up. But I think you get my point. The more you look for something and the more you praise yourself for looking for it, the more you will automatically and habitually look for more of it. Look for things that make you smile and laugh and you will soon become optimistic and happy just by virtue of the fact that you are developing a happy habit.

When you smile, something magical happens. It's instantaneous. Your smile is like a virus, infecting everyone around you. Every single expression you make with your face carries with it a biochemical change in your body. It causes your brain to release signals and compounds that make you feel a certain way.

Feeling good is linked to a smile and feeling bad is linked to a frown or a scowl and every variation in between. When we smile we cause ourselves to feel happy. Your smile also affects others around you. For the most part a smile will soften others when they see it. Isn't it true that you can actually tell when someone is smiling even when you hear them talking on the phone? And when you do, doesn't it make you feel a bit better just for listening. And when they chuckle or laugh we can hardly keep ourselves from smiling or laughing a bit along with them. Try this out sometime. Smile while you are talking to someone and notice their demeanor changing as you carry on the conversation.

If Talk Is Cheap, a Smile Is Cheaper

From a scientific point of view, when we smile we increase the level of electromagnetic energy that we emit from our bodies. This can be witnessed through photographic imagery where you can actually see the energy that anything living generates. When we are frowning, or negative, stressed, angry, or anything negative, the energy is reduced. When you smile, on the other hand, and truly feel positive, it impacts your health and appearance, and attracts people to you. We've all had the experience where we feel someone looking at us from another car, even with the windows rolled up and the stereo blasting, we feel them looking and we look over at them.

Consider this. There are some 43 muscles in the human face, most of which are controlled by the seventh cranial nerve (also known as the facial nerve). This nerve exits the cerebral cortex and emerges from your skull just in front of your ears. With each expression comes a chain reaction of moving parts that produce chemicals that cause us to feel a certain way.

Stimulate your nervous system!

Chapter 7

YOUR LIFE

"Don't cry because it's over. Smile because it happened."
—Dr. Seuss

» **CREATE YOUR MAGNIFICENT DAY**

» **START LIVING IT**

» **GET HAPPY, AND STAY HAPPY!**

You can't hide anymore!

And you don't want to. So let's get up close and personal. This is me you're talking to. You picked up this book for a reason. And even if it were just out of curiosity I'm going to assume that you are open to the possibility of a bit more happiness in your life. Even if you are already happier than a kid on Christmas day and you just want the information so you can teach it to someone else, I'm also going to assume that you want some sort of change.

What you focus on is what you get.

Just by reading the information contained within these pages, you WILL change and as a result you will automatically affect those around you. You're going to go further, faster. So in keeping with the process that I outlined in the previous chapter I'm going to help you learn a bit about you. It's time to get dirt honest with yourself. And in the process, you're going to learn how to GET happy now and STAY happy for life.

Step 1: Starting Point

The first step, as I outlined in the prior chapters, is called Destination, Navigation, and Justification. That refers to the process of getting from Point A to Point B. The first part of navigation is the starting point. Point B: Where do you want to be? Where do you want to end up and what is your destination?

Said differently, What do you want?

I can't tell you how critically important this is to your success in anything, including your happiness. It is the number one most important element in the whole process. It is, however, amazing how many times people miss this altogether. More people know what they don't want then what they do want. People can describe in great detail what it is that they have and want to avoid but spend very little time on the real deal of what they really desire. And for the most part it is because they don't really know.

I grew up in a small town in the Mojave Desert. The roads were straight and went on for miles without stop signs. Three or four times a year you would see on the news how someone was driving out in the middle of nowhere and crashed into a telephone pole. And if they lived they would always say the same thing. "Last thing I saw was the pole. I didn't want to hit the pole." But they would always hit it.

They even shot aerial photos of the stretch of deserted road and it showed that 90 percent of the skid marks went right into the poles. This fascinated me because a pole is only a foot and a half in diameter. Why did they hit the pole when they knew it would probably kill them and everyone in the car? The answer is simple and it sheds a big bright light on how we all function as human beings.

Whatever you focus on is what you get. It's what your body is drawn to. *The people who hit the poles hit them because they were looking at them.* It's that simple. Whatever we look at with our eyes closed or open is what our bodies will do to get there. And the more emotional we are while we look at it the more committed our physical body is to making it happen. It doesn't make a difference whether it's right or wrong, good or bad; it just works that way. When they are looking at the pole their mind becomes locked into that destination and the body does whatever is necessary to go get it NOW! It's not about knowledge or right or wrong or logic. It's purely psychological and physical. In this case the brain is triggered by the sight of the pole (visual) and the body is triggered by the brain to behave by steering into the pole. When people tell me what they don't want, it's like looking at the pole and screaming, "I don't want to hit the pole!"

Instead of looking at the pole, look at the space. And your body will assist you in getting there. It's where you really want to go anyway and perhaps the coolest part is that it is generally a bigger target. When you aim for the space called your specific happiness you delete the poles in life and become focused on where you are going instead of where you don't want to go. I hope you can see that this is the same thing that you are doing and have been doing your entire life anyway. So now you'll be using it and directing it to bring you to the happy instead of all of the other stuff that lines the path.

The Answer Is to Look Somewhere Different!

I can't tell you how many times people have come to me seeking a change and they sit there in my office staring at me with a smile on their face and hope in their hearts that I can help them feel better and move on with their lives. But as soon as I ask them what it is that they want that look turns to shame, pity, anger, frustration, or sorrow, followed by some horrible tale of a terrible thing that happened to bring them to this point. They were happy and good and in an instant when I asked what they wanted they'd go into a nosedive. I would ask again. "What do you want?" Then with some surprise and hesitation they would proceed to tell me in a different way what they didn't want. They'd say, "I'm unhappy," or "I'm scared all the time," or "I'm depressed," or "I'm angry." Then I'd ask again, "Okay, what do you want?" "I told you. I'm upset, I'm scared."

It amazed me how very few of them could ever articulate what it was they wanted. How can you get where you are going if you don't know what you want?

I even had one guy tell me these exact words: "Depression washes over me like a scalding hot wave of debilitating emotion that drains the very bone marrow out of my soul." He had studied his horror to the point that he had a well-defined, practiced description of what it was he didn't want.

As you will soon find out those words carry with them a chemical release that causes people to feel even worse. After a few times of asking what they want and I would tell them no, you are telling me what you don't want and that is a huge reason why you have exactly that. They always then look at me like an innocent puppy with its head cocked to one side. Tell me what you want instead of all that crap. Like clockwork their eyes roll around in their heads and they would become speechless. If they did come up with something they would guess at it and make it up there on the spot.

This would tell me that they don't know what they really want and because they don't know what they want they are wandering around in confusion and hoping something will come along and guide them. So I hope my point is clear. We will be systematically finding your destination!

Believe me, when I was homeless I didn't know what my destination was and couldn't envision how to get there if I did. If you feel overwhelmed, just listen, press on, and do the assignments. Don't put the book down! It's a living tool, and it's like having a personal trainer right in front of you. I was once unfocused, and now I've got so much clarity about my life that I set goals and achieve them. I rarely miss the mark. When I set New Year's resolutions or life goals, I mean it. I know I'm going to reach them!

Know Where You Are Now

The second piece of the navigation process is to know where you are now. This is equally as critical because this is where we will calibrate what we must adjust and how much. We can map out our journey in the most efficient way. It's like when I go shopping with my wife and we look at the kiosk map in the mall. The little arrow says: YOU ARE HERE. Then, we check out the path to the destination, and of course as a guy, I just want to go directly from Point A to Point B and get what we need. It's a direct path! But I've discovered that women (in general) are different. At least mine is. My wife won't just buy. She shops. And for her the process of shopping is stopping, browsing, socializing, and taking indirect routes and surprising detours along the way. But for the purpose of this book, and your results, I'm going to respectfully ask you to think like a guy. No matter what your gender, think in a direct navigational path that will get you the results you desire, faster.

So now let's start the process with a few exercises for you to do. They are simple and should take you only a few minutes to complete. Unless I tell you to take longer I want you to spend only about ten to twenty minutes at a time, maximum, on each of them. The reason for this is I don't want you to overthink things. We have found that overthinking all too often produces paralysis by analysis. When you write, just write the first thing that comes to your mind. You don't have to be poetic or well-versed. You can always go back and doctor it up later. The important thing is just to get it out of your head and onto paper. And I do mean paper. You can write here in your book or write in your journal; either way, I want you to write. NOT JUST TYPE. When you physically write you are fully engaging your entire nervous system. You are certainly welcome to transfer your work to your computer later but for now please go old school with pen and paper.

An Exercise: Your Magnificent Day

Our first exercise in this chapter is to outline your magnificent day. This is the Point B, the destination, the place you'd ideally like to end up. Think big! The sky is the limit. In fact, there are no limits! This is an open-book assignment, and I think it'll help you get clarity about your own life if I'm open about mine.

I was given this assignment years ago and I took it to heart. At the time my biggest passion was music and my biggest outcome was to have a recording contract with a major recording company. I had been working really hard for some time and I was miserable, stressed, and almost burnt out. I was up to my spleen in debt and working ten hours a day as a dental technician. I wrote down what I thought at the time would be an absolutely magnificent day.

I let my imagination go and dreamed big—if money were no object and I was getting all that I wanted and felt as good as I could on that day three years away. I then gave it to someone and they were to mail it to me in six months so I could see how I was doing on my journey. Then I went about doing some of the things that I am going to have you do in this book.

Here's what I wrote.

> Joseph's Magnificent Day is:
> I wake up, energized, refreshed, and excited!
> I take a breath and think about the day ahead.
> I look back over my life and smile because
> the journey has been challenging but I have
> grown and learned from each step. I'm
> grateful beyond measure and I'm thankful
> for all the blessings in my life. I stand up
> and get a feeling of absolute gratefulness,

happiness, contentment, and joy.

I am especially excited because this is the day that I sign my new recording contract with a major recording company and begin my new journey to complete my dream. I get out of bed and immediately go into my own personal recording studio and slam out yet another magnificent song. As the day goes on I am blessed with good friends and family contacting me and me them. The signing goes spectacular and my producer and managers and the rest of the team and I celebrate like crazy. I enjoy a wonderful dinner with my girlfriend and at the end of the day I'm sitting in my dream car staring out the moon roof looking at the beautiful full moon.

Using the method that we are going to do now, I embedded this vision in my subconscious and as a result became increasingly more confident and happy. I became more ambitious and willing to work harder for what I wanted because I had that image firmly planted in my subconscious. It became the space between the poles.

For the next three years I moved several times and changed addresses each time. One day three years later while sitting in my car in my driveway sorting out my mail, I came across a letter with my own handwriting on it. The original address was one that I hadn't lived at for three years! The envelope had several red stamps on it, indicating that the recipient wasn't at the address.

When I opened it I realized what it was and what had happened. It was the letter that I had written three years prior. It had been mailed to my old address six months later but I had moved. The letter went from house to house following me all over the place until it finally wound up in my hands on that day. And here is perhaps one of the coolest things that happened. It was on that very day that everything in that letter had happened almost to the tee. I had signed my first recording deal, I did at the time have a recording studio in my home and all of the events described in the letter had happened. I was almost in tears as I read it and when I got to the end my hands were trembling as I looked up to see a beautiful full moon through the moon roof of my bad-ass car. Too cool, huh?

Now I'm not promising that this will happen to you but what I am saying is that when you do it you will feel better and you will follow the plan you create. You've got to envision it to achieve it. You've got to envision it to activate your brain and your body to bring you to it and it to you. It makes no difference whether it's a material thing or an emotional thing. It's all the same to the brain. You've got to know exactly what you want and where you are going, in order to get there.

Take a moment to complete this important exercise for yourself NOW.

You can write right here in this book or you can do it in your journal. Either way, put pen to paper. Do it right NOW. Let your imagination go and have fun!

If money, time, and resources were no object, how would your own magnificent day look, taste, feel, smell, and sound like?

Even if you just list things, it's okay. Don't worry about being grammatically or politically correct. This is for your eyes only.

Don't worry about what we are going to do with it, just write and have fun. Write it as though you already possess it and you are living it.

You could write:

> <u>My Magnificent Day is</u>:
> "I'm healthy, happy, and full of joy and excitement. I smile most of the time and I'm excited about the future to come. I'm enjoying the energy that I have and the friends that I have the privilege of being in my life. I am grateful beyond measure for all of the many blessings that I have in my life and I am ecstatic about the ones to come. My greatest joy is helping others see their happiness and I glow with positive energy and expectancy."

Be creative. You can't do this wrong unless you don't do it at all. Use your imagination and stimulate that wonderful brain of yours.

My Magnificent Day is:

_____

_____

_____

_____

_____

_____

_____

_____

_____

_____

_____

_____

_____

_____

There… now you have it. This is what you want, at least in this context. Whether or not you get all of the things that come along with that day in terms of material things, wouldn't you agree that the feeling that comes along with this day is what you ultimately want? So for the time being, we will use this as your outcome. Well done!

I'll guide you, but you've got to agree to take the reins of a bright new future and hold on! If you haven't competed the exercises on the previous pages, go back and do them now! Pause. Take a break. Get a pen. Flip back through the pages and fill in the blanks. I'll be right here waiting. If you've already done the exercises, let's move on.

Step 2: Where Are You Now?

In order to get where you want to go you need to know exactly where you are now. After all, you can call a taxi on the phone and tell him where you want to go. But first you need to tell him where you are so that he can come and get you. You have to give him the exact address and location that you want to leave from. This next part might be a little uncomfortable but remember you are the only one who needs look at this. Also remember that it is imperative that you be dirt honest about this both good and bad. Write the first thing that comes to your mind. If you find that you are padding your comments or holding back, then rewrite it. Remember you are programming your nervous system by doing this so you might as well do it right.

Answer the following questions and comment on them as you do. In your current day to day life, how would you describe yourself, your life, and your lifestyle?

How happy are you on a consistent basis?

1	2	3	4	5	6	7	8	9	10

What is your level of happiness? On a scale from one to ten, with ten being smiling ear to ear, giggling, and happy like a five-year-old on Christmas morning. And one being depressed out of your mind, face down in a gutter somewhere, crying yourself to sleep every night with a bottle of Jack Daniels and a gossip magazine. How would you score yourself?

What is your level of unhappiness?

1	2	3	4	5	6	7	8	9	10

On a scale from one to ten, with ten being livid enough to lash out and hurt a five-week old puppy and one being just a little annoyed, how would you rate your average level on unhappiness?

What percentage of the time do you spend unhappy? (or angry, frustrated, sad, depressed, hurt, feeling taken advantage of, jealous, etc.)

10%	20%	30%	40%	50%	60%	70%	80%	90%	100%

Describe yourself when you are feeling unhappy. (or moody, angry, moping around, blaming others, solitary not wanting to be bothered by others, indulging in mind-numbing behaviors like drugs, alcohol, TV, Internet, etc.)

_____

_____

_____

_____

_____

What percentage of the time do you feel spiritual? (or enlightened, worship conscious, connected to your higher self, peaceful, etc.)

10%	20%	30%	40%	50%	60%	70%	80%	90%	100%

Describe yourself when you are feeling spiritual. (or light and easy, calm and centered, compassionate and living, etc.)

_____

_____

_____

_____

_____

What percentage of your time do you spend happy? (or excited, giddy, laughing, in love, admiring, content, joyful, etc.)

10%	20%	30%	40%	50%	60%	70%	80%	90%	100%

Describe yourself when you are happy.

_____

_____

_____

_____

_____

_____

_____

_____

Remember, this is going to be your menu to choose from later. So please take the time to do this exercise. It doesn't matter if you're the CEO of a corporation or an executive, or a stay-at-home dad. It doesn't matter if you're female, black, white, or Peruvian. You can be happier and achieve sustainable success!

If I would have had a mentor to walk me through these exercises when I was at the lowest point in my life I would have gone further, faster. It wasn't until I started on the path of self-improvement that I sought out mentors like Anthony Robbins, Deepak Chopra, John Grey, General Colin Powell and other great minds that I was able to transform my thinking. Today, we're igniting a change in your heart that will help you go further, faster. Once you've completed the magnificent day exercise, you'll start seeing, perceiving, and feeling the world differently.

Chapter 8

WHY
(THE MAGIC MAGNET)

» **DISCOVER WHAT REALLY DRIVES YOU**

» **MAKE DECISIONS FROM THAT CORE**

» **LIVE INTENTIONALLY**

He stepped onto the stage with all the swagger and style of absolute royalty. This was a dream come true and he had worked his whole life to get to this moment. And what a moment it was.

He and his band had the coveted slot as the opening act for one of the world's most famous and celebrated groups. The energy, passion, and anticipation crackled like electricity in their hearts as the announcer introduced their set. The audience screamed. He felt in his heart that that he was one of the greatest guitarists, singers, and songwriters of all time.

The lights came up, the band dug into their instruments and the speakers thundered with sound loud enough to move a planet from its orbit. They rocked it! But instead of cheers of approval and adoring appreciation what came back from the crowd was a smattering of horrible jeers, boos, and disgust. The boos from the audience grew louder with every second until finally they were drowned out by the thunder of the sound system. They couldn't deny it, they couldn't go on. It was over. They left the stage after only three songs and the artist was devastated. Within a few short minutes his dream had turned into a horrible nightmare!

On October 11, 1981, at the Memorial Coliseum, Prince Nelson Rogers opened up for the Rolling Stones and was booed off of the stage. Following that dreadful day, the press was ruthless and the news spread like wildfire. Even Keith Richards of the Rolling Stones took shots at the young performer.

For most this would have been the end of their career, or at the very least a real good reason to give up. But something inside was pulling him to push on. Something that empowered him to give what happened a meaning that would electrify him to be and do more! Within two years Prince was dominating the music scene with an innovative, unique sound and style that no one saw coming. He upended the world of music and never looked back. His style and music forever changed the face of music and he is one of the most prolific and talented musicians of our time. In 2004 he was inducted into the Rock and Roll Hall of Fame.

What is it that pulled him forward?

What causes his psychology to make sense out of what others would call a disadvantage? One might think that he has something special that makes him go above and beyond, that he is so talented and gifted that he surely must have a unique ability that most of us don't. Prince has the same quality within him that you and I have, which is what I call Internal Pull. And it came with the package for every single one of us at the moment of conception. It's that God-given thing in your DNA that your father and your mother passed on to you. It is the spark of life that makes you do what you do each day!

The Pull toward Greatness

This navigational pull functions 24/7 in your subconscious mind and lives in every single cell in your precious body. The cool part is that we can harness that great power and direct it and utilize it to our advantage. We can tap into it and ride it like the Lone Ranger rides Silver. It's your reason why. Why you are doing what you are doing is a direct result of your internal pull mechanism. It's how we justify our behaviors internally and externally. In an instant we will rationalize our way of making sense of the actions that we take, whether they're good or bad. Your entire nervous system will align with this justification and make you feel like you must do what you are doing. It will override logic and reason and it will conquer fear. It will solve problems and motivate the soul to take action.

Most people approach challenges the same way. They try to figure out how they are going to do what they need to do, or how to fix something or how to solve the problem.

You will find a way to make it happen if you have a strong enough why. When we find our WHY and attach our outcome to it we stimulate our nervous system to find a way as well as ignite our energy to do what it takes to make it happen. When you do this, your entire being will engage to make it happen. This is what makes you get up early and stay up late to get something done. It works both ways. It is the grind behind your bad habits and destructive behaviors.

Chances are you want to become happier, stronger, wealthier, or simply more content on a daily basis. But everyone needs a reason to pull them forward. I like to use the following example in my books and seminars to illustrate the importance of the WHY. If you want to create lasting change, find your reason WHY. If you want to help someone else transform, help them first understand their reason WHY they need to.

Imagine for a moment you see a house surrounded by a moat full of water. In that water are alligators, sharks, poisonous fish, poisonous snakes, leaches, and flesh-eating piranhas, and the moat is surrounded by a ten-foot barbed wire fence with barbed wire on top so you can't climb over and two hundred and forty volts of electricity surging through it. On the fence is a big bold sign stating that anyone caught trespassing beyond the fence will be prosecuted within the fullest extent of the law, and in the process receive a full-on, hardcore, L.A.P.D. beat down!

You and I are standing outside of the fence looking in. We can see the shark fins in the water and hear the crackling of electricity surging through the fence. And I say to you that inside the house, in one of the bedrooms, lying on one of the beds is a brand-new, crisp one hundred dollar bill, and if you can get into the house, you can have the money. Well, I can assure you that even if you're homeless, you're not going to think the risk is worth it. You value your life over the money, and you'd say, "No way, Joseph, keep the money!"

BUT, if I told you that inside the house, lying on the bed in one of the bedrooms is the person you love the most in life, and he or she is fast asleep and the house is on fire, that changes things. The person you love is at risk for losing their life, and suddenly you've got a reason to get into that house. No matter what the risk, you'd want to try.

In fact, ask any firefighter who has witnessed it and you'll find that you would fight me or anyone else who tried to stop you from getting in there. Your endorphins would kick in, you'd have a supernatural burst of energy, and you'd become superman! Or superwoman. You'd get resourceful, creative, and you'd think of things you never thought of before. You'd react with a sense of urgency as your body rushed forward on autopilot toward your goal of rescuing the one you loved!

Your drive and determination would be maximized, and your focus would be razor sharp—*all because you now have a strong enough reason WHY.*

Although this is a pretty radical and morbid example, my point is to illustrate that this is how we, as humans, function. Just like the pole example in the previous chapter. It has nothing to do with logic or intelligence or right or wrong. It's purely psychological and physiological. We are wired to go beyond what we believe is natural to achieve! So why don't we? Most of the time, it's because we don't have a force to propel us forward. Without that internal desire, or pull to stimulate the nervous system to do more, we just don't. But when we get emotionally committed and attached to our reasons why, we find a way to get it done.

Real Life Application

I hope you can see how powerful a piece this is and how understanding and applying this concept to your life can produce remarkable results. That is exactly what we are going to be doing as we continue our journey to a happier you.

Many life-change books focus on strategies that impact your mind. And that's not a bad thing. The mind is an important part of your body! Other books focus on diet or physical fitness. But the truth is, you can't separate the two. Your body and mind is one connected organism, and both influence the other. This is a book that focuses on both. I want to present the science behind why we think what we think, and do what we do, in order to spark inside of you lasting change.

In this chapter, we are setting the foundation to move forward. *I want you to come up with a strong reason why you want to be happy.* Why you are willing to go the extra mile to live in a happier state. It can be for your health. It can be that you want to set a better example for your children or family. It can be because you want to feel better and you deserve to do so. It can be that you want to be a better person for the one you love. It can be that you want to do it for yourself.

I want to be happy because: (e.g., I'll be a better dad, a strong leader, a good mentor)
Find your own reason why. It has to be authentic.

_____
_____
_____
_____
_____
_____
_____
_____

If you need to go back and review the things that you wrote down when you described your magnificent day, go ahead. Think about why you want this day to be like that. Again, don't overthink it, but do allow yourself to over-feel this one. Dig deep and find a reason for doing something different and unique. Think about how your life will be different and how this will help you. What will you do differently? Who will it matter to the most? Who will be a part of your life and the way you will change? It is okay to have several different reasons why. If you do, write them all down and then prioritize them. Which one is the one that you have the strongest emotion about?

Remember: You can focus on specific images and words in your mind. Instead of random, unintentional thoughts coming in you can build a life of intentional thoughts that help you to create intentional outcomes.

The Facts about the Science of Happiness
Throughout this book I'm focused on guiding you through the right steps to get the right results. Here's what science has shown:

1) Studies of centenarians across the world show that happiness is the key to longevity.[1]

2) Happy people are more likely to give back to the world, which in turn, increases happiness.[2]

3) Happiness increases nearly every business and educational outcome: raising sales by 37 percent and productivity by 31 percent in corporate studies.[3]

4) Your body is composed of billions of cells, and each cell needs a combination of different nutrients every day in order to do what it is designed to do. It's important to eat right, think right, and take action. Happiness is the key to the wellness in all other areas of your life.[4]

5) Happy people have more overall physical fitness and emotional wellness.[5]

6) Happy people make more money![6]

Take some time and write your reasons why. Write as much as you can.

I want to be happier so that I can:

_____
_____
_____
_____
_____
_____
_____
_____

What is it inside your heart that pulls you toward the future? What reasons did you list for wanting to become happier?

The thoughts in your brain are frequently changed with new information, but there are also belief systems lodged in your heart. What makes you tick, gets you jazzed, excites you, and creates energy, pulling you toward your goal? Everyone is different, and we all have varying desires, needs, and goals. I'm passionate about people, motorcycles, music, family, and sometimes even my dog. You're passionate about other things, and each of us has varied degrees of intensity and emotions. The things I feel are important, you may not. The things you value as a priority, others may not. That's the magic of our uniqueness. That's why this book is all about you. If you found it hard to come up with something, go back and just do it! *Do not skip this exercise.*

It's important to make changes that stem from your own intrinsic desire, and not someone else's. This is YOUR life, not your uncle's, not mine, nor your mother's or father's. It doesn't matter what your best friend thinks, or what his or her goals are even for their own life. All that matters is what YOU want, because the only way to get a positive outcome is to start with authentic input in the first place. So let's get to it and accelerate. We are now going to go further, faster.

Chapter 9

GO FURTHER FASTER

"Just do it."
—*Nike advertising campaign slogan*

» **BE COACHABLE**

» **ELIMINATE TOXIC THOUGHTS**

» **LIVE TODAY WITH INTENTIONALITY**

Your body is an amazing specimen, and it's more sophisticated than a computer. Your heart pumps on average 1,500-2,000 gallons of blood through your body every day. You're composed of veins, arteries, muscle, cells, tissue, and nearly 60,000 miles of blood vessels! And your brain is just as magnificent.

Within your anatomy you've got an advanced microprocessor of a brain with vast capacity for gathering information. You also gather data through each of your senses, and this process goes on continually as you take in information by sight, smell, listening, and touch. With all of these things coming at you at once, plus the messages from the outside world, it's easy to get confused. And that's what this living tool is about. Within these pages is the secret to unlocking a life you deserve.

Because no matter how smart you are or how sophisticated our brains were wired to be, we cannot achieve what we desire unless we just DO it. That's the beauty of simplicity of the Nike ad campaign years ago that seemed to speak volumes with just a few simple words. Just do it. Stop talking about it. Stop dreaming it. Stop planning it. Just DO it.

One of my favorite quotes is that on the eighth day God said, Hey, I've been working for seven days straight and I made all this great stuff for you. Now do something with it. Don't make Me come down there!

How Your Brain Processes Information

In addition to all of the subtle messages you get from dreams, the words of others, billboards on the highway, and everyday encounters, your brain is integrating all of that data with your prior experiences, which we call memory. It's a fine balance within your system, as all of this information arrives and affects your sensory perception.

Even the way your memory works is remarkable! Imagine your brain housing a large filing system that can be utilized to recall memories and experiences and information for learning a skill or a job. All of these facts exist in your database! Some data is stored in your short-term memory, some in your long-term memory. Some is stored and utilized later in the day.

At times, human error occurs because unlike a computer, our storage and retrieval processes are mixed with judgment, rationalization, and experience and are limited to human knowledge and application. It's not possible to make the right decision all the time, but it is possible to build a stronger foundation to go from.

The thinking process is the process of associating one's imagination and internal conversations and references to a specific focus and then drawing conclusions. Meaning, when we focus on something we make pictures and words in our minds that are related to that particular focus. If you are thinking about a car you are making images and words associated to that car and then concluding what it means and what to do about it.

This is the mind-body connection. That's all you need to know. And here's the cool part. That's all you need to know to be happy too.

If thinking makes the body do certain things and the heart feel certain things, then all we have to do is think the thoughts that produce the happy stuff. For example, there is a nerve originating in your brain called the vagus nerve. The nerve extends from the brain stem all the way to the viscera. The word *viscera* refers to all internal organs in the chest. The vagus nerve transmits signals to and from the brain, helps control muscle function, heartbeat regulation, and other important services. What does all this mean and what does it have to do with being happy? It's simple. What you think determines what your body will do instinctively. This nerve is only one of the many connections within your body. It's easy to see why our stomach churns into knots when we are worried about something.

Eliminate Worry When You See It or Feel It

Worry is a focus on the negative, with concern that it will happen. The negative chain of worry causes the brain to release signals to this nerve to make your stomach dance, heart race, and breathing quicken. Perhaps the biggest discovery with regard to the vagus nerve is the connection to the heart. For all practical purposes our feelings are associated with our heart. When you feel love you feel it most in your heart. When you feel sorrow, sadness, joy, empathy, or any emotion it is felt in the heart. Scientifically, this all makes sense if you look at the truth that the heart and brain are connected from the start, as one cell in the embryo. The heart and brain are both connected, from the start, originating from the same cell. As the heart grows it separates and becomes its own organ.

There's a reason Proverbs 4 says guard your heart, for it is the wellspring for which all life flows. Your life energy flows from what comes into your mind and takes root in your heart. If it's stressful thoughts you're allowing in, you increase cortisol and stress hormones.

The best news about all this is that we can alter how we think and change the entire chain reaction. We can do it in the moment and we can do it in such a way that it becomes a natural default.

Anatomy of Human Thought and Behavior

INPUT Something happens that stimulates one or more of our five senses.	Visual .... Sight Kinesthetic .... Touch Gustatory .... Taste Olfactory .... Smell Auditory .... Sound
THOUGHTS We automatically react with thought to make meaning of it.	Words and images that represent the input.
PHYSICAL REACTION Our body reacts to the meaning/thoughts with physical movement.	Breathing, heart rate, hormone release (adrenalin, endorphins, etc.), eyes dilate, blood pressure, movement, digestion, etc.
EMOTION/FEELING We respond with emotions that support the thoughts and meanings.	Joy, excitement, fear, anger, love, doubt, disappointment, etc.
ACTION/ACTIVITY We respond by doing something to support the emotion.	Fight or flight, get out of bed, exercise, speak, make a call, eat/diet, hesitate, procrastinate, etc.
RESULTS All actions will produce a specific set of results.	Income increase, weight gain/loss, etc.

Study this diagram until you really get the flow of what happens inside of your brain and your body. It's a simple process, and when you understand it you will see how behavior can be predicted. The brain and body are connected. If you can control what goes into both, your chances of happiness, fulfillment, and success can be increased.

Truths foundational to this process:

» Behavior can be predicted with a high degree of certainty.
» Action and outcome can therefore be predicted.
» You can use tools and skills to redirect
   and shape your emotions.

Look at the diagram again, and notice that there are two main touch points that you can impact that will interrupt the chain of emotion to create a different result.

One touch point is *physical.* The second is *thought.*

> Physical Input
> We can deliberately cause physical input to create specific thoughts. It's not hard to figure out that we can literally do something to simulate each of our five senses. You can intentionally look at a specific thing to establish your mood. You can taste, smell, touch, and listen to calming music, for instance, to sleep. You can listen to hip hop or rap or pop to work out or increase energy. Those are examples of using physical stimulus to impact how we feel, eliciting a physical reaction that affects how we think and behave.

This is good news because it is as simple as setting up your immediate environment to supply those types of physical input. I will be telling you about how to do it in the pages to follow. For now, just understand that you can take control of that part of your life almost immediately.

Thought Patterns

The second area of impact is in the area of thought. Your thoughts consist of images and words. Normally these images pop into our minds randomly or from external areas of influence such as media, music, billboards, people, places, or things. However here, right now, we are talking about a different process entirely.

In the empowering process you're about to go through, we are beginning with the knowledge and understanding that you can focus on specific images and words in your mind. Instead of random, unintentional thoughts coming in you can build a life of intentional thoughts that help you to create intentional outcomes.

By doing this you will override the physical input and affect the subsequent links in the chain. This may seem a bit more complicated than just changing the physical things that are around you but in reality it is easier. Once you learn how to do it you can direct your thoughts immediately. 2 Corinthians says "Take every thought captive." It's a proven concept, as old as the origins of time. It works! Yet only one percent of humans actually use it as a weapon to win in the battle of life. In this process I'm teaching you, you're in control and you can do it in a way that it will become an automatic response. You won't have to consciously do it. It will happen on its own. This is something called conditioning and we do it all the time anyway. It is the way you have learned anything that has become a habit or skill. We do it deliberately and quickly.

Capturing Joy and Happiness

Now you're going to learn how to use an amazing tool. This is something that will provide benefits for the rest of your life. How would you like to have a way of instantly creating a resourceful state of mind and attitude anytime that you wanted or needed it? This is a tool that works for you even when you don't know it is working. It's a tool that you will sharpen automatically, and develop subconsciously so that it impacts your nervous system. This will allow you to build a powerful storehouse of emotions that you can tap into anytime you want.

It's like taking out the garbage. We will eliminate toxic, unhappy, and negative feelings but that leaves a big gaping hole if we don't replace it with something positive right away; you will either go back to the old way of feeling and thinking or you will seek and find something else to replace it with. People who have addictions to sex or alcohol do the same thing. They give up alcohol but replace the addiction with smoking. Both can kill you. *Our challenge here is to replace your negative feelings with positive ones.*

And the challenge with that is that there is always an endless flow of negative influences disguised as good in the form of TV commercials, media, and gossip-based rhetoric that will occupy your time and send you down a nonproductive path. We want to overcome any distraction and break that pattern.

We are working toward conditioned response, or as it's known in the psychology field, anchoring.

Basically, it's important for you to know that most things happen subconsciously. The things that go on in your underlying emotions and brain and heart affect the way you act. Most of it occurs subconsciously. Ninety percent of how we react is conditioned response.

You may remember a case study taught in your high school or college courses about Pavlov and his dogs. It's an overused, over-referenced study but it's an important way to remind you of how conditioned response works in your body and mind. It still is a very important discovery, even though it occurred in the 1800s.

The Russian psychologist Ivan Pavlov was researching the digestive tracts of animals. He noticed that he could link different stimuli to the hunger states of dogs, and found that if he rang a bell whenever the dogs were in a hunger state, that later on, after the dogs were fed and full, he could ring that same bell and the dogs would go into the hunger state again. The hunger state would produce the physical reaction of salivating. Even if the dog was asleep, it would salivate as though it hadn't been fed for days. Pavlov performed this experiment for years with dogs and other animals and concluded several things. He found that:

» Most living things with a heartbeat share the same type of nervous system regarding our association of outside stimulus to our subconscious and involuntary behaviors, including human beings.

» By applying any stimulus during the time that the subject is at the peak of any emotional state one can link that state to the stimulus applied.

» The stronger the emotion the quicker and deeper the anchor will be.

» You can add to and build on any stimulus response to create an even stronger and deeper association and emotional response.

» The effect of this process will last indefinitely until it is replaced with another stimulus.

In the experiments, the bell that Pavlov used is called an anchor. An anchor can be anything that produces a specific emotional response.

If you think about it you will see that your whole life is full of anchors. Humans are often referred to as stimulus-response creatures. Something stimulates any of our five senses and we respond accordingly. Think about it. Isn't it true that whenever you hear a horn honk you immediately become alert and more aware?

When you are driving and you see the red brake lights of the car in front of you, your mind immediately becomes alert and your foot jumps to the brake! It's an instantaneous response. Or perhaps you smell a certain cologne and it reminds you of someone special, and you smile or relax. Or perhaps you smell vanilla, and associate it back to your mom's cookies or pies. Realtors often ask their home seller clients to bake cookies and leave them in a kitchen before a showing. The goal is to elicit a positive response and a warm feeling when the home buyer comes through.

The emotions I describe in the scenarios above were brought on by the stimulus of the sight of the red brake lights or the smells of the cologne or vanilla. All responses were brought about in the same way. We are unconsciously (without thinking) triggered, just like Pavlov's dogs, to feel and respond in the same way that Pavlov triggered the dogs to salivate. That is how we learn and live and respond, subconsciously.

When the red traffic light flashes on you don't have to think to yourself to take your foot off of the accelerator and put it on the brake. It happens automatically. This holds true with most of the things that we do in our day-to-day lives, including being happy and joyful. The good thing is that we don't have to think about it before we react. Otherwise we would waste a lot of time and could be in a lot of danger if we had to take the time to think about jumping backward up on the curb when we hear the horn of an oncoming bus. The nervous system has already been programmed to react on its own because it was trained to know what to do when it hears that sound!

The best part about being stimulus-response creatures is that we can deliberately program ourselves to react to a specific trigger or anchor with any emotion we desire. The behaviors that are attached to that emotion will automatically occur.

We can program ourselves to respond any way we want and can do it quickly and easily. What this means is that you can learn to create an automatic feeling and behavior that you can use anytime you want. And perhaps the coolest thing about it is that it will become a part of your belief system and the nervous system will rewire itself to accept it as who you are and how you behave.

Triggering Your Emotions to Happy

So how do you produce the emotions that you want to use in this triggering process?

The answer is to think, and you will then feel. When you think, you create a picture and words in your head. If you remember from our earlier chapters this is the thinking process and our bodies will respond to those thoughts with movement. It's unconscious and unavoidable but predictable. Since our minds and bodies can't tell the difference between what is real and what is imagined it will treat the thought as real and react and respond accordingly. And while we are feeling those emotions if we apply any stimulus with intensity, the emotion that you create will be automatically linked to that stimulus. If you remember a time when you were laughing and allow yourself to really feel it and while you are feeling it you tug on your ear lobe or say the word *green* or ring a bell or anything at all, you "anchor" or connect that created emotion to the input. You can literally use any of your five senses as a trigger.

Other ways of creating emotion are listening to music or moving your body in a certain way like dancing or exercise. Watching movies or actually having a real experience. All of these things and many more will produce emotions that are favorable and as soon as you do if you apply the stimulus while you are at the peak you will be adding to the trigger.

I call it being an anchor hound.

My silly dog Winston sleeps like a log for several hours of the day. But as soon as he goes outside he is on full alert. He sniffs anything and everything, looking for something new. Even though he has been in the same yard all his life he looks for something new and expects to find something new every day. When we take him on walks he is the same way. He's looking for something new and exciting. I've taken that cue from old Winston and applied it to this process and my life.

The Happiness Process

One of the assignments that I want you to do is to search the world for things that make you happy and feel good. Search for things in your past and your present. Make things up for the future. Look for a flower or an attractive person or listen for good music or beautiful smells of your favorite foods or fragrances. Seek places that make you feel relaxed and whole. And when you feel the effect of those situations simply smile and say thank you.

The smile will be your physical trigger and the thank you will be your auditory trigger. Think about it; won't it be powerful that whenever you smile you recall powerful emotions of joy and happiness? And every time you say thank you, you feel grateful and peaceful. I also want you to pinch your right thumb and forefinger together as though you are picking up a penny or pinching yourself. Do it for one full second while you are feeling the joy of the thought or memory. By doing this you will be combining two of your most powerful senses. Your auditory when you speak the words "Thank you" and your kinesthetic when you pinch your fingers together. You are also engaging your physical body, and that we will discuss later, but it is powerful. What would you do if you had this tool? How would you use it? What differences would you make in your life?

It may sound simple but it's the secret to real life change. Instead of living on autopilot, you take control and life with intentionality. Instead of just being a responder, you live life with purpose, and harness every aspect of your mind.

Here is a simple process to create your own emotional trigger. It will be personal to you and it will be your own special sanctuary that you can use any time you want. It will only take you about ten minutes. The process goes as follows.

Step 1.   Write down as many things that you can think of that make you happy, memories, and things that you can think of that bring joy to you. Write things that make you laugh. Remember times in your life that you laughed and giggled. Write things that make you feel connected and loved, peaceful and grateful, any and all things that make you feel good. This will be your menu to refer to when you are triggering yourself.

_____

_____

_____

_____

_____

_____

_____

_____

_____

_____

_____

Step 2.   Find some music that inspires
you and makes you happy.

Step 3.   Turn on the music and review your list one by one.

Step 4.   As you remember these times allow yourself to
get lost in the memories and allow yourself to
feel great. If it's difficult, just change to something
else. Go to the next thing on your list.

Step 5.   At the peak of any emotion apply the
stimulus. Simply smile and say the
word "Magnificent!" out loud.

Repeat this process through your whole list and at the end praise yourself and move on about your day. Don't worry about whether or not it is working. You just about can't get this wrong. About the only way that you can get it wrong is by not doing it at all. Remember this is how you have been conditioned throughout your entire life and will continue to be. All you are doing is harnessing emotion and directing it along the path to produce the positive results you want.

Remember, we are talking about ultimate, destined, unadulterated happiness! We aren't talking about a forced feeling, temporary excitement, or momentary joy. We are going to create sustainable, lasting happiness and contentment that becomes the undercurrent for who you are and the life you want to live. And that's the secret. Happiness doesn't have to be dependent on your life circumstances. It's not a condition that's contingent upon how much you make or what you do or even how handsome you are. Happiness is in the mind, and you have the power to multiply it. This is your opportunity to step up and take the bull by the nose ring and lead it to the water and make it drink.

In this next chapter, I am going to add to the arsenal of tools you can use.

Chapter 10

WALK YOUR THOUGHT

"No man can walk out on his own story."

—Rango

» **BE ANYTHING YOU WANT TO BE TODAY**

» **ANYTHING IS POSSIBLE!**

» **IDENTIFY THE TOP 5 REASONS YOU AREN'T LIVING IN ULTIMATE HAPPINESS**

Anthony Robles was born with only one leg.

Imagine the moment in the hospital room where the new mother is handed her bundle of joy, and the doctor has to deliver that news. Every parent expects their newborn to be like everyone else's. Two arms, two legs. But that wasn't the plan for Anthony.

As the years passed, he learned how to do things that the other kids could do, and he didn't let anything stop him. He learned how to play, participate in sports, and excel in school. His mom was an encouraging force! She told him he could do anything he wanted to do, and in 2011 Anthony Robles, a wrestler at Arizona State University, won the college wrestling NCAA championship!

"I grew up believing that I can do whatever I set my mind to," Anthony said.

Can you imagine the fortitude?

It's all about changing your perception of things. Dale Carnegie said it's not who you are but how you think that makes you happy, and he was right. The choice is yours.

Greatness is inside of you, and it's up to you to live it. You can be absolutely anything you want to be, TODAY.

You don't have to look far to see examples of amazing people who have bounced back or redefined their adversity. One is a man who was born with no arms and no legs but now has a global business where he travels to countries across the world!

When Australian Nick Vujicic was born, his mother was so shocked at the way he looked that she couldn't bear to hold him. She asked the doctors to take him away. Can you imagine that kind of rejection? The shock of seeing her newborn arrive with no arms and no legs was simply too much for her to handle. She was devastated, confused, and unable to process it.

But years later, when Nick came to her and told her he wanted to be a motivational speaker, she supported him. His friend had just taken him to a seminar given by a motivational speaker, and he knew right then that that's what he wanted to do with the rest of his life. He believed in the dream first before anyone else did. Today the 28-year-old speaks worldwide to audiences in packed stadiums. In Mexico he addressed an audience of 100,000. He has 40 million hits on YouTube, has surfed with Bethany Hamilton—the real person portrayed in the movie *Soul Surfer*—met world leaders, and dined with Sir Richard Branson. He travels to Brazil, Singapore, India, and Romania with his team of managers and handlers on a schedule and pace hardly any able-bodied person could keep up with, but his physical condition doesn't stop him. Nick says that the key to his happiness is understanding his calling. He knows without a doubt, as he works in schools and talks across the globe about bullying and suicide prevention, that he was created to do exactly what he is doing.

But look at the odds of that occurring. Why would someone

with such a glaring disability choose to speak in front of live audiences, when he could simply utilize the technology we have today and work from home? He did it because it was his destiny, and his gift. He didn't let any obstacle or physical disability stand in the way.

When you consider the lives of these young men, one black, one white, one American, one living in Australia, you begin to see that anything is possible. If someone without a leg can compete against athletes who've trained their entire lives and win a national championship, you can do anything you want. If someone without any limbs at all can become a world-class spiritual teacher who exemplifies how people should never give up, there's no dream you can't conquer!

It's All How You Look at Things

If you see things from a nothing-is-possible attitude, nothing will be possible. If you see things from an anything-is-possible attitude, you can change the world!

Deep down you've probably got a desire to be happy and make a difference in the world. You deserve it, and you know you can achieve it. So what has prevented you from achieving your dreams thus far? What keeps you from achieving what you long for in the core of your soul?

The Vital Next Step

Let's move on to the next step in our process.

Now that you have a better feel for where you are and where you want to go, let's peel back some more layers of the onion and discover what really has gotten in your way. What has stopped you from being happy or productive and more optimistic?

Remember that this step is a vital piece of the puzzle. This is also the part that most people avoid at all costs because it may be uncomfortable. I encourage you to step up now and get strong and be honest. If it does get uncomfortable just take a deep breath and recognize that this may be the last time that you feel this way at this level and that your reasons for doing this are to achieve the outcome of being and feeling more joyful in your life.

Brands, Companies, and Even Countries Are Built on Stories

Your story is worth a fortune. Companies build entire brands on them. Starbucks prints powerful, life-impacting quotes or poetic statements on their paper cups at certain times of the year. When you walk into a Starbucks you see words and art the walls, and hear funky music. You can purchase CDs at the counter, along with your latte, from an off-the-grid barista with a nose ring. Apple culture is the same way. It screams, We are not like most companies, we are different! Both companies are creative types, preferring their story to be told as one of innovation, versus tradition. If you've got pink hair and tattoos you might not get hired at IBM or Microsoft, but you might get hired at Apple.

Companies intentionally build a story around their brand. For years numerous articles were written about the story of Bill Gates, the Microsoft founder, who dropped out of school. It was that story which gave everyone a reason to cheer on the CEO, the company, and the products to greatness. Since the dawn of human existence people have been telling stories—stories of bravery, failure, love, triumph, defeat, and every conceivable configuration possible in between. And through the interpretation of those stories we allow or disallow ourselves to be moved forward or backward. We all have thousands of stories about ourselves and our experiences throughout our lives. We all tell stories to ourselves. Ninety-five percent of the time they are being told in our subconscious mind and we are not even aware that we are doing it.

The second interesting thing is that with each of those stories comes an emotional response/reaction, which means that we are constantly reacting to the stories being told in our subconscious mind. (Don't worry; I'm going to simplify it all in a moment.) But because the human brain and nervous system generally can only handle a few things at a time it has developed an ingenious system of categorizing, organizing, defining, and prioritizing all of the stories. For the most part these stories are organized as past, present, and future.

The way the brain determines which ones of these stories to pay attention to and which ones will be moved to the top of the priority sequence is through the meaning we give those particular stories. The meaning we give a story is based on the amount of emotional intensity we have about that event. The more emotion we have attached to that story the higher it moves on the list.

The meaning we give things is not always logical. It doesn't always make sense. We make the decisions subconsciously on which stories and events are important to us based on the amount of emotional intensity we have about those events.

This is how we learn and grow and this is why something that can seem small for one person is a huge deal for someone else. The meanings we give things are based on the amount of emotion we had before, during, and after those events that the stories are about.

And to top it all off we will make up meanings to support our feelings. What does this mean? Like the guy taking the pill in the movie *Limitless*, who doesn't really live in one reality but several. He takes the pill and it makes him stronger, faster, and better able to see the unseen, learn foreign languages in three days, and operate at superhuman levels. But it's temporary. And it's not real. When I was living in my cardboard box I didn't eat sometimes because I couldn't afford to, and my mental state was one of a starvation and desperation, and along with the hunger I felt terrible.

I felt terrible! But what if I'd created a different story at that time, about others who fast and don't eat out of choice, creating a nomad-type story around my situation where I was an Indiana

Jones-type survivor foraging for food? I may not have had food but perhaps I would have felt better and gone and done something about my situation instead of floundering in my misery. Your story determines your path. It's up to you to create it.

What's Your Reality?

Are you seeing things the way they are, or were, or have you attached a different meaning to the story? Something horrible could happen to someone and they feel anger, frustration, and shame and become disempowered. That same thing could happen to another person and they make it mean something that empowers them to be brave, courageous, resilient, and strong! The word *bushido* is derived from a traditional Japanese samurai term, which means authenticity, honor, courage, and heroism. No matter whether your day is filled with meetings, presentations, or time helping others, you can change another person's life by being a heroic warrior.

Whatever stories you have created for yourself are still being told every day in your subconscious mind. They are shaping your very existence on the planet. Most of them are not true and applicable anymore and are using up valuable space on your pristine hard drive of life.

If you think of yourself as a warrior, you will be. If you tell yourself a story that involves a victimization theory, where you can't get out of your situation because you're handicapped by life or circumstantial events in some way, you will be handicapped. The garbage you allow into your mind can hold you back. As you travel through this process it's important to monitor the garbage that comes in. If you've been wronged, or are in pain, be quick to discard it, and like a writer, rewrite your story.

Your Personal Story Has Power

Think of the negatives that come into your mind as garbage. If the garbage truck dumped a truckload of garbage onto your front yard and left it there, you'd have to deal with the stench of it for days and possibly even weeks. Eventually the garbage would reek so bad that the neighbors would complain. It would rot and fester, and infiltrate the air and soon everything around you would take on the odor of the garbage. And this is the way it is with the toxins we allow into our minds. It doesn't matter if it's from the Internet, a posting or message from Facebook or Twitter, an email, or a phone call. Sometimes we even create the toxic messages ourselves.

On the other hand, if you think of yourself as a joyful, compassionate, loving, fun, and energetic person and you tell yourself stories that support that thought then the exact opposite will happen. You will fill your reservoir with magic honey that strengthens everything that it touches and enhances your entire life. Either set of stories can be true or false. The choice is always yours. But the one that is told the most is the one that you will believe the most.

One man's adversity is another man's treasure. In the book *The Problem of Pain*, C.S. Lewis wrote that "pain provides an opportunity for heroism," and it does. You can bounce back from a painful situation and transform the world! Ask any divorced couple why they split and you're likely to hear two different realities. Are we living in virtual reality? Or real reality? Sometimes it's hard to tell. The smartest, most successful people are self-aware of what reality is. They don't tell themselves stories that hinder them. Or they correct it when they do.

It's Never Too Late for a Course Correction

This book is a living tool, and you can use it like a U-turn sign on the highway. By now you may have a fluttering feeling rising up in you that there are things you've believed that simply aren't true. You've created stories or mini novellas about your life, or the way others have wronged you, that have negatively impacted your relationships. Maybe you've even subconsciously sabotaged your happiness.

Perhaps the coolest thing about our humanness is that we can change the meaning of any story to make us feel good and empowered and happy! Let's do this. Right now. If you're the CEO of a company and you feel a great responsibility as a leader and because of that you're already stressed, the exercises within these pages can shift your mindset. If you're an executive within a large company, the exercises can transform your soul.

You just have to be committed to resiliency no matter what. If you feel like you've failed, get back up! Bill Nguyen, a multimillionaire CEO of startups across the globe, has won and lost millions of dollars in his various technology ventures. His creation, Forefront, was sold for $145 million. Another venture, Lala, Bill sold to Apple for $80 million, but other companies he started lost millions. He doesn't get devastated by his failures and keeps a positive attitude instead. Bill says, "I can outlast anyone. I'm like a roach." Because the story he's told himself is one of resilience and strength, Bill cannot be defeated, even when his ventures fail!

How about you? What story are you telling yourself? A perfect example is what I told you at the very beginning of this book. For several years of my life I defined the story to mean that I was worthless and hopeless. I wanted to hide the fact that I'd been homeless. After all, who wants to highlight their biggest failure?

But I have given it a new meaning and that story empowers me now! It's important to reframe the event.

There's true power in the human story. Everything in life, in fact, revolves around story—music, songs, romances, and businesses. Life is built on the stories we tell and continue to tell ourselves.

Stories are how we support our reasons for why we don't do what it takes to get what we want. If someone says that they aren't happy because they were abused as a child, it's a story they've created.

All they are really saying is "the story that I keep telling myself about what happened makes me feel bad and I have told that story so many times to myself that I don't even hear it being told anymore but I still feel bad." Now this, of course, is an oversimplification but I think you get my point. My point is not to make light of or negate that terrible things happen to good people. It's just that in most cases the memory of what happened and the meaning that one has given that memory is what keeps them from creating the emotions that they really want to have.

So having said all of that, let me ask you a couple of really important questions:

What are the top five reasons you aren't living in the ultimate happiness that you desire?

Here are some examples.

> » I own a company and my staff drains my time and energy.
> » My husband/wife is driving me crazy.
> » I'm living paycheck to paycheck and
>   I'm in debt up to my spleen.
> » I worry about my health but don't have time to work out.
> » I'm stressed out of my mind and I have
>   too many things on my plate.
> » My sales team won't make their numbers!
> » My boss sucks.
> » I was teased as a child for being too shy and
>   now I can't make friends because…
> » I'm afraid to approach people.
> » My mother is sick and I'm worried about her constantly.
> » I'm getting old.
> » My business is taking off but I'm concerned about finances.

Take the next few minutes and search your soul. Come up with at least five of your own reasons that you are not as happy as you could be. Don't hold back and remember if you get uncomfortable or bogged down just stop and take a deep breath and recognize that this is all a process. This book is an interactive tool.

It's important that you do this right now. Stop and do this simple exercise now and you will be adding to your foundation.

And if you can't think of anything then make something up or guess at it. You will know if it is the real deal as you try to make it fit. At the very least it will get your memory juices going and lead you to what you truly believe.

Be descriptive.

I'm not as happy (or living in my ultimate peak performance) as I could be because:

1. _____

_____

_____

2. _____

_____

_____

3. _____

_____

_____

4. _____

_____

_____

Now choose the one that sticks out the most—the one that you have attached the most emotional intensity to, the one that you feel the most resentful or frustrated or helpless about. Don't overanalyze it, just look at them and choose.

Rewrite this reason here:

_____

_____

_____

_____

_____

What Is Your Story?

Now describe the origin of this reason. Where it started; how it came about. Be as specific as you can.

Even if this is the first time that you have ever written it out or spent this much energy, please go for it full-on now. What is the story behind this incident or event that has impacted your life? If you were going to be paid for this story, what would you write?

Here is a short example:

> My name is Janet Smith. Five years ago I was on my way home from my acting class and I stopped at Starbucks for a quick latte before I hit the books for my exams the next morning. I ordered my drink and met a man in the line behind me. He had gorgeous eyes and was tall, dark, and unbelievable. We sat in that Starbucks until it closed and then we went to an all-night diner and talked until the sun came up. His name was David and from that night on we were inseparable. We were so in love nothing else mattered. I never felt so safe, so alive, as when I was with David. Then one day I got a call from my best friend Gena. "I hate to be the one to bring this to you Janet. But David is seeing another

woman." I was angry that she would even suspect my prince charming of such a terrible thing. But when she emailed me the photos I almost died right there on the spot. There he was kissing and caressing some blonde. A piece of me died that day and I can never trust another man. I try to be happy but my heart is broken into a billion pieces and I can't put them back together.

Now you try it…

If you need more space, enter it in your journal if you haven't already. And again, do not move forward until you have finished this assignment.

My story is:

_____

_____

_____

_____

_____

_____

_____

_____

_____

_____

_____

_____

_____

_____

_____

_____

_____

Hopefully this process has stirred up some things in you.

The Mental Bait and Switch

Now it's time to change the meaning of your story because it's never too late to have a happy childhood. One of the first things that I learned from the book *Think and Grow Rich* by Napoleon Hill was that for every action there is an equal or greater reaction. The same holds true for experiences in life. For every adversity there is an equal or greater benefit.

Here is your chance to dig out what yours is.

Keep in mind that the process will work even if you aren't sure of what to do. Also, these things that we are doing now are just the pieces of the process and not the complete process. So stay with me and hang in there.

Remember what I said was so cool about our humanness? We can change the meaning of anything to suit our outcomes. I don't expect you to change anything right now. Just come up with a better meaning for the story that you just wrote. You can rewrite the story and make the words different but most important is to take something of value from the experience. This isn't a book, but a living tool. It's like six months of therapy for the mind. If you're not willing to do the work here, it won't work. Please don't trick yourself into thinking you don't have the time to do this just because you feel a little uncomfortable. It's meant to feel uncomfortable.

What did you learn that would make you feel better about what happened?

_____
_____
_____
_____
_____
_____
_____
_____
_____

And what is a better meaning for it all to have happened in the first place?

_____
_____
_____
_____
_____
_____
_____
_____
_____
_____
_____
_____

It's time to reframe your story.

In my case I carried the fact that I was homeless as something to be ashamed about for many years. Too long! Up until about 12 years ago I didn't talk about it to anyone. Most of my friends and even my long-term friends who knew me back in the day never knew.

When I first did this exercise I changed the meaning to something that empowered me, and it changed my life. I now believe that had it not been for my experience I would never have met the old man in the welding shop. I would have never gotten the book *Think and Grow Rich* and I never would have found my true calling and I never would have been able to give back to as many people as I have been able to thus far. And I'm just getting started!

So take some time now and think about your new meaning. Use your imagination and make something magnificent. Remember that you made up the meaning you've had for all this time and you believed those lies. So as long as you are going to make stuff up you might as well make up some really cool and useful stuff. It doesn't have to be complicated, deep, or profound.

What benefits can you take from your experience that you have already used to your advantage? What great things have come from you having gone through what you went through? How are you different for the better from it? Who else is better from it? Even if it is something as simple as at least you got it out of the way and you don't have to learn that lesson again. Just make it mean something that feels good and is better than the crap you came up with before, even if the meaning is that at least that is over and done with and you learned to be wiser in your choices in the future.

Just like the previous exercises, do not go further until you have completed this assignment.

The benefits I have chosen to take from my experience are:

_____
_____
_____
_____
_____
_____
_____
_____
_____
_____
_____
_____
_____
_____
_____
_____
_____
_____
_____
_____
_____
_____
_____
_____

Getting to a positive outcome involves being open, honest, and self-aware. Once you take the time to go through these exercises and really think about where you've been, it'll be much easier to accelerate to where you want to be.

Chapter 11

THE HAPPINESS PROCESS

"Even if you are sitting on a gold mine, you still gotta dig."
—*Mike Wang*

» **SEE IT, SAY IT, MOVE IT, PROVE IT, GROOVE IT!**

» **DO IT EVERY DAY**

» **WORK THE PROCESS, CHANGE YOUR LIFE**

This is the part of the book where the rubber meets the road. This is the place where we are going to literally install happiness into your very nervous system. You will program yourself to default to optimism and happiness. We are about to blow your mind, body, and heart. You are going to literally change how you feel going forward and ongoing.

Keeping in mind that knowledge is only potential power and action has the tendency to produce temporary or short-lived change, it is imperative that you employ the philosophy of activity. Activity of course is repeated action until one surpasses their goal. You must participate in creating your desired outcomes. I'm going to guide you through exactly what to do, and you must do it if you desire the result.

Most people don't realize that you can rewire your brain. But you can. It's actually possible to interrupt previously existing thought and behavior patterns, grow new neurons, and condition yourself to think and feel differently. Neuroscience proves it, and economists, psychologists, medical doctors, educators, and sociologists have studied the benefits for centuries.

This chapter focuses on a specific action plan to implement over the next ten days. And here's how it works! Water, weed, fertilize, repeat. The repetition of the steps in the process is key and will compress the time it takes to reach your goal! What you do while you repeat is called rehearsal and every time you rehearse it drives the lesson deeper into your nervous system. As we build up the muscle memory in your brain, it establishes a pattern that eventually becomes second nature.

Why Is That So Important?

When you start DOING this process, and working the steps over the next ten days, you'll find that soon it's nearly impossible to get into the negative. That means any negative beliefs or stinking thinking simply will evaporate over time. And even though you will start to feel the effects very quickly, you must keep going with the process. As silly as it may sound, I'm going to have you try to feel bad so that you can feel good.

It's a reversal process. Remember wax on, wax off—a forward momentum of reversing damage.

You can reverse all kinds of things, including lung disease when you stop smoking, unhappiness, negative thinking, aging, and debt. Think about executives and entrepreneurs like Donald Trump who reversed debt to achieve millions again. We can reverse things we didn't think were possible. Medical doctors report that smokers who stop smoking can actually repair and rebuild damaged lung function within a matter of months. Lung cancer can be reversed, and so can aging and brain function and many other things. Some people look better at fifty than they did when they were thirty. The good news is it's possible to reverse unhappiness too. And perhaps even more exciting and beneficial, you will boost your happiness tenfold in the process.

Drawn by the Future versus Pulled by the Past

The success in this process is that you are being pulled forward by a new future where you are light, optimistic, and happier, rather than driven by past events, thoughts, emotions, or obstacles. Once we identify whatever hurdle, limiting belief, or fear that's hindered advancement to that highest level of contentment and happiness, we can soar.

In seminars I tell people to bring me their worst nightmare, their worst memory or the thing that bothers them the most, the feelings that stop them from going after their dreams. I tell them this in the pre-work so that they will have contemplated it for a while. Without fail, they never let me down. They bring some pretty heavy stuff with them, things that all but tear your heart out, stories of abuse and sorrow and heartbreak and torment. It doesn't matter if I'm speaking in Finland, London, or America. Everyone has a story.

I tell them to bring these feelings because in a very short time they will no longer be able to feel that way. And it won't be something that I do, but rather something that I will teach them to do for themselves. And they will. And they are amazed because within five to seven minutes they cannot feel the negative emotion anymore. Once we delve into it they've learned the strategies to go beyond it.

This Process Is about Happiness, Not Trauma

So don't feel that you have to dig deep into your past and find something that tears you up. I'm sharing the experiences of others so you can see how effective it is on things as radical as trauma, so it will be a piece of cake for what we want to accomplish here. The great part about this is that it is ongoing. I am teaching you how to use a living tool that will condition your nervous system so that it becomes so natural that eventually you won't have to do this over and over again. The other thing to understand is that this process has what we call a global impact on all emotions. What this means is that there are only good and bad emotions, only empowering and disempowering. There are varying degrees of both but no in between.

So when you affect one emotion or memory it affects the whole range. Meaning that if you choose a memory or emotion that causes you to feel fear and you lessen the feeling associated to that particular memory or event, it will lessen your levels of fear overall and heighten your levels of courage. That's why I sometimes refer to it as the emotional bait and switch. It's kind of like fishing. When you put your hook in the water, you put bait on it in order to attract fish. If you don't bait the hook, you don't get anything! In this process, you bait the bad to come out and wreak its usual havoc. When it's out in the open you obliterate it and switch it with something good.

The Happiness Process:
See It, Say It, Move It, Prove It, Groove It
It's simple.

> **Step 1.**   See it
> (see and feel the negative).

> **Step 2.**   Say it
> (say your key word to interrupt the pattern).

Step 3.   Move it
(move your body to widen the gap
and prepare the nervous system).

Step 4.   Prove it
(stimulate the positive emotion
and place it in the gap).

Step 5.   Groove it
(praise and repeat; do it over and over again).

In More Detail...

The *See It, Say It, Move It, Prove It, Groove It* process goes as follows.

First, block out at least ten minutes where you can be alone and undisturbed. Find a quiet place where you can make some noise without anyone interrupting. It might be a closet or a bathroom. It might be somewhere outside. Eliminate media. Turn off phones, televisions, computers, and anything that could distract you. Be willing to be silly and have some fun!

Second, choose a key word to interrupt your pattern. It can be anything that causes you to shift your focus and arrest your feeling. Make it fun and even silly. You can say "hello," "wait," "wake up," "love," or even "pizza" or "cake." Anything! So long as it is strong and different. If you are having a hard time coming up with a key word, just use "STOP." And, it is okay to change your key word later, just use the same key word all the way through each session before changing it.

Step 1.   Stimulate the un-resourceful feeling. While in a seated position briefly imagine the feeling that you want to replace. It can be the same as the feelings that you wrote about in Chapter Four. It was the thing that stops you and hinders your progress in terms of happiness and feeling good. You can also just imagine yourself unhappy. It is not necessary to feel it deeply, just the beginnings of it. The first time is the longest but as soon as you feel any part of it (*this will bring forth the negative*), then…

Step 2.   Abruptly say your key word out loud. You can even shout if you feel so inclined. The more radical the better. (*This will temporarily interrupt the negative thought and emotional pattern and obliterate the feeling /pattern and create a scotoma.*)

Step 3.   Immediately jump to your feet, shake your body out and take a deep breath (*this will widen the scotoma and create a mental vacuum*), then…

Step 4.   Put the biggest smile on your face, snap your fingers and say the word "MAGNIFICENT" out loud. (*You will have stacked up several happiness anchors that will fill the void when you fire off the anchors in that moment.*) Because your brain and your nervous system were forced to operate in a vacuum, they will be searching for something to fill that gap. This is where you will be inserting your new happy and positive feelings. And because you have built them up from the past, they will come quickly without you having to search for them. It's way cool!

Step 5.   This last step in the process is what I call "Groove It," which is simply celebration with praise. When you praise yourself, you lock yourself

into the process of thinking differently. Do
a little dance, make a little noise, get down
tonight. Shake your butt, pat yourself on the
back, say something cool to and about you like
"I freakin' ROCK!" (my personal favorite).

Repeat steps one through five 10 times; each time you will notice that it will be harder and harder to feel and bring up the negative.

As you go through the *See It, Say It, Move It, Prove It, Groove It* process, do it naturally and move on with your day. Your nervous system will do all the rest of the rewiring work for you. Just have fun and be authentic.

The Time Is Now!

Now is the moment to change your life forever. It's all up to you, and with this process no one else can do it but you. Sometimes you just have to take matters in your own hands. Forget about the past and any failed attempts at chasing happiness, and don't let that be a barrier to success.

See It, Say It, Move It, Prove It, Groove It works! I've heard all the excuses in the world, when coaching people across the world to live happier lives, and I've seen those same people actually restored, happy, and revitalized once they listened and implemented this process. I've seen people who were paralyzed with fear and depression quickly turn their lives around and become functioning, happy members of society. I've done it with rooms full of thousands of people, dozens of languages, and scores of different cultures. I've seen men whose careers were stagnant take off like a rocket to become millionaires. I've seen the most depressed, pessimistic people you could imagine restore their hope and optimism. It's all up to you.

Your future lies in your own hands! So just do it. If you think it's too hard, let me share an inspiring story. And as you read it, just imagine what fear, challenge, or problem you would like to obliterate for yourself… because now you can!

In 1998 a man called me for some coaching. He was calling as a last resort to a lifelong challenge: a fear of heights. Specifically, a fear of high bridges. He explained that he could have gone his whole life and lived with his fear by simply avoiding any and all high bridges, but something important had come up and he had to overcome his fear (his block) immediately. Needless to say, he was scared and extremely unhappy.

He explained to me that his passion was cooking and that he had recently landed his dream job in a posh hotel restaurant on Coronado Island just off the coast of San Diego, California. The problem was that to get there on time he had to cross the Coronado Bridge (there is access via a peninsula but that was over an hour's drive, which wasn't acceptable to him).

I was living in San Diego at the time and I knew of the Coronado Bridge. It is an awesome example of engineering and towers several hundred feet in the air. It's tall enough that people have parachuted off the sides into the bay. (There are signs prohibiting this now.)

This man had received my contact information from my friend Anthony Robbins. He was desperate for help. I could tell by the tone of his voice that he was scared. I really wanted to help him and knew I could. The challenge was I was due to get on an airplane and fly to Australia in just a few hours. I had no time to see him. He begged and pleaded with me but there was no way that we could meet. So I told him that I was going to teach him something over the phone for ten minutes, and if he did it, he would have no problem getting over his fear.

What I taught him was basically the same process that you have just learned. I was a little more intense, of course, because of the nature of his challenge. But for the most part the mechanics were exactly the same. We practiced the above process a few times.

He actually started feeling better right then and there over the phone. I told him to keep it up for ten days, giving him the same schedule that you now have (see the BONUS Appendix). New challenge: It was Friday night and he said that the next time he had to go to work was on the following Tuesday so he wouldn't have ten days before he had to face his fear. I said, "Then you had better get on the ball!"

The following Tuesday while I was in Australia I called home to check my messages. There was nothing out of the ordinary until I got to his message. He was yelling, screaming, and actually crying with joy! He had just gotten on the other side of the Coronado Bridge and he was ecstatic. He said that he had done the exercise twice as much as I had prescribed (since he didn't have ten days) and had no fear or problems going over the bridge. He said that by Sunday night he was actually getting excited to cross the bridge and even contemplated going over it that evening just for the heck of it.

Perhaps the coolest thing about this story was an email I received from him several months later… with a picture of him skydiving! The look on his face was of pure joy.

This Happiness Process you're embarking on is simple and powerful, but *you* have to do it. If you want it done right, you have to do it yourself. I'll guide you, but you've got to agree to take the reins of a bright new future filled with abundance. What you have learned so far is the foundation for the rest of the journey.

The time is NOW!

Chapter 12

THE HAPPIEST PEOPLE IN THE WORLD

» **DETOX DAILY**

» **GUARD YOUR HEART AND MIND**

» **LIVE AN ANYTHING-IS-POSSIBLE LIFE!**

Think about the happiest moment of your life, the moment you were in full-on joy! It might not have been an event, a rush of adrenaline, or even a fabulous trip to an exciting destination. It might have been a simple joyful moment outside, with the fresh air blowing gently and the rays of the sun washing over you. This kind of happiness just flows through, washing over you like a cashmere blanket. It's comforting and warm, and sometimes unexpected. It can't be bought on or provided by alcohol, shopping, or some other event. It comes from a place deep inside.

The happiest people in the world live in this state of mind.

By conditioning the body through the see it, say it, move it and prove it process, you are creating and utilizing a stimulus response mechanism that puts you in this happy state of mind. It's no different than building strength or muscles through lifting weights at the gym. It works. Science has proven it. Only here what we are doing is stimulating strength in our thought patterns.

You're programming your subconscious to react. But your subconscious is making decisions anyway so you might as well direct it in a controlled pattern, versus allowing it to run wild like a little child in a sandbox. Your life is too important to leave any stone unturned. Most people allow their subconscious minds to make reactionary decisions. What you've learned here will change all of that.

Remember Step 1: Destination (Navigation) from Chapter Five, and how in order to get where we are going we must first know where we are and where we want to go. Navigation is going from Point A to Point B.

I'm reminding you of this to eliminate the negatives in your life right now and detox from every prior way of doing things, including all the garbage you used to allow to flow inside your head from the phone or email on a daily basis, and get really focused on what you want. Do a detox daily. Living happier means being more aware of what's coming into your mind and heart.

We've already passed through the justification stage. You know what your *why* is.

Remember, I'm your coach, and this book is a living tool. Recall your *why* now. It is time to get centered on what you want, why you want to be happy, and the reason you'll internalize this process even after you put down this book. What's your big WHY? Remember it now. It's your pulling force.

Gratefulness

About six years ago I was hired to do a series of talks to a large company here in the United States. The company had many, many branches in several states across the nation.

The project consisted of me traveling to several of their larger locations and working with the CEO and upper management and designing a program for the 4,500 employees and staff throughout the company. It all culminated in a large company event where they brought in all of the top achievers as well as several thousand distributors and employees and celebrated their successes and laid out the plans for the company's future. After speaking at that event I was asked if I would do a companywide conference call as a follow-up to my talk at the event and the material I had prepared for the organization.

When I asked them what they would like me to talk about to their entire company the director said, "Just talk about what you think is the most important thing for them to practice now in order to make their work lives go better and for them to be happy."

At 7:00 p.m. I was informed by the call director that there were 2,300 people on the line and growing. We waited another three minutes and I began to chat. My topic was "Gratefulness as your key to fulfillment and happiness." The talk lasted about an hour and then I opened it up to questions and we stayed on for about another hour. Just like this book, I don't believe that words alone and inspirational stories are the real key to creating measurable change so I always provide something to do along with the knowledge that I share. That way the audience will have a tool that they can use to get results rather than just having a good time being inspired.

So I talked to them about the obvious benefits of gratefulness and how it was the antidote to any fear or negative emotions, as well as how to construct gratefulness (which is basically the same way that you are learning how to construct happiness) and even a schedule to practice and rehearse so that they have more in their lives. When the first part of the call was finished the operator announced that she had twenty people in a queue waiting to ask questions and that all of the other lines were full. I'm always delighted when there are a lot of questions because it usually means that they are genuinely interested in getting a result and not just listening for the sake of listening.

All of the questions were great but there was one in particular that stuck out and I remember because she asked if I could hear the sounds of relief and agreement from the other open lines. I could tell that others wanted to ask the same question. She asked, "Mr. McClendon, you keep saying live our lives with gratefulness instead of being grateful. What is the difference between being grateful and gratefulness?"

The answer to that question pertains to living happy too. Because although being grateful is fantastic, it generally pertains to being in the moment. It's generally experienced for that specific moment or moments and then it's off to the next feeling.

But gratefulness is a perpetual state experienced on an ongoing basis. It's a consistent disposition where you are constantly experiencing the feelings of thankfulness and gratitude. In short, gratefulness is ongoing gratitude.

Months later I attended a church service with some friends and the preacher explained how she'd heard a speaker once (turned out it was me!) talk about Great FULLness. She said at first she thought he meant gratefulness but he kept emphasizing GREAT FULLNESS. She said that he explained that gratitude is just an emotion and that all emotions are manufactured. He said that if we keep in our minds the images and the words that represent what we are grateful for and we keep a smile on our faces then we would be experiencing gratitude, and that if we repeated this process with enthusiasm, then it would take hold and we would become more happy, productive, and grateful feeling. He said that we could make any emotion our default. She said that she was so intrigued that she even asked a question at the end of the call. "What is the difference between being grateful and great fullness?"

What she said next felt like she had peeled the top of my head open and filled it full of joy. She said he explained that we should live our lives full of greatness. Full of the pictures, images, sounds, memories, and movements that are great and we will feel great and grateful. Even though I didn't remember putting it like that she got that message. And in fact she was teaching me and a whole room of others from what I had taught her. And perhaps the coolest part about the whole thing was that no one knew it was me. Not even my friend who had invited me to the church. She then told us that the speaker had given everyone a simple assignment to do and that she had taken it to heart and did it and that is why she was so happy and grateful that day. I was elated, being that my ultimate outcome is to impact as many people as I possibly can in a positive way. She was doing it with her enthusiasm.

I share this story with you because I want you to get that the message of gratitude is so important. The emotion of gratitude is the one emotion that will slay any dragon of fear instantly and that if you practice it you will become it and it you. All of the physiological things that I talked about in earlier chapters will come to your side and assist you in your ultimate outcomes. The great news is that the processes that you are doing in this book will cultivate gratitude. So I say to you as the preacher said to us all, live your life with GREAT FULLNESS. Full of the thoughts words and movements that embody who you are.

Real-Life Application

Here's an example of real-life application of how the process of interruption and anchoring works:

Let's say I wake up feeling grand, and shower and shave. I work out, and then someone pulls out in front of me on my way out of the gym, cutting me off. It makes me angry, triggering a memory of a time when someone else took advantage of me, or when a woman at the grocery store did the same thing and I let it go. But this time, I'm angrier. Because the anger from before resurfaces.

Then I think of a time when an old girlfriend told me I was

too passive, which only adds fuel to the fire. As the person in the parking lot at the gym speeds ahead of me, I recall a recent memory of when my wife nagged me about where to park, even though I was in the driver's seat, and I tense up even more. This is not a real example, mind you, but it certainly could be. All of those memories, triggers, and recalled emotions lie in my subconscious in a dangerous cocktail of bubbling anger and rage!

Suddenly, I want to speed up and get around that car in front of me. I want to take control, fight back, and do something so ridiculously outrageous like flash an angry hand gesture as if I'm fifteen, shout out the window, or pull in front of them! Yeah! I want to show them who's boss.

And that's often what happens when we feel anger. (Think about the incidences of road rage where people actually get shot while driving!) The factor we see is when old, stored emotions add up and get stacked on top of each other.

But with this process, you can start to SEE the emotion before it's enabled and full-on, and your subconscious will INTERRUPT the negative response and events from occurring. You drive along, get cut off, smile, tug your ear lobe, and even (if jokingly) say the word "magnificent!" and the subconscious angry flash of emotion that was a pattern throughout your life is interrupted.

Change = Power

If the definition of power is the ability to change (and be resilient!), then it means that intelligence, knowledge, and information are not enough. At best they are just potential power. If you have been doing the exercises in the previous chapters you have all of the puzzle pieces that you will need to create the happiness that you picked this book up for in the first place. And you have a strong association to the word *magnificent* and the great feelings from the things you listed and a smile on your face. Even if you don't think you do, if you have been doing what I asked, you still have it and it will serve you.

Think of it this way: We all know things but we don't always apply what we know. With the best of intentions for whatever reason our psyche rationalizes, deletes, distorts, and justifies our behaviors that hold us at the threshold of happiness, achievement, and success. That's like repeating the same bad behavior over and over again and getting the same results.

If it's weight that we want to lose we know how to lose weight. There are thousands of diets out that work and millions of people who have done it. The know-how is there. Know-how is a plentiful commodity. What is not so plentiful is something called wisdom. Wisdom is applied knowledge. Wisdom is knowledge utilized until results occur. And the only way to get wisdom is through experience. So that is what we are about to do. We are about to put together all of the puzzle pieces and perform a strategy that will produce results.

The Subconscious Mind

Tons of information resides in the subconscious mind. Each day you're getting bombarded with messages, texts, twitters, Facebook updates, images from electronic ads, magazines, billboards, and television, among other things. All of these images and messages tell you what young, sexy, healthy, and strong looks like. But what if a lot of what you've heard and taken in is garbage? What if some of the messages you've received are toxic, instead of true?

Let's say you are at work, and an email pops up that offers a statistic about aging.

It gives you a test to determine your real age, and you follow it down the rabbit hole until you've taken the test, forgotten about the work project or email, and now you're thinking about how to be younger. Let's say the email ad tells you that a lack of vitamin E causes wrinkles and poor skin tone. Instinctively you desire vitamin E and soon you get up and drive to the pharmacy on your lunch break. And what do you buy? Vitamin E. You bought into what you read. It might be true or it might not.

But we do these things in the rest of our lives as well. We make decisions consciously, and also subconsciously. Many people have subconscious addictions without even realizing it. A woman sees a magazine of a celebrity wearing a blazer and jeans and later she buys a blazer and jeans. The same thing happens over and over again, because the outfit makes her feel good—because of the positive emotions associated with the picture she saw. The linkage is between the pretty celebrity in the magazine photo and the purchase. A week later she sees another photo of a celebrity wearing a bracelet and buys the same thing. It's a trend. A week after that, as fall is ushered in, she sees a magazine of her favorite celebrities and models wearing boots with fur, and decides she wants a pair. Soon her husband discovers she's in debt and has racked up thousands of dollars in credit card debt unknowingly, and the truth is, the woman didn't even realize what was happening. There are subconscious drivers pushing your decisions.

The pleasure stimulus occurred in the buying, and the woman in the example above felt a release in some way after she had the outfit (which she thought made her look more attractive). We don't view this stress, pressure, pull, pleasure seeking, action, relief process as addiction but in reality this is the subconscious cycle of addiction.

In subconscious marketing, a new field has emerged. Major companies are now aware of the power of the subconscious mind. This gives even more validity to everything we've been discussing here, in this book. Major corporations like Coca-Cola and Frito-Lay have hired companies to study the way consumers buy. One firm, NeuroFocus, is a California-based neuromarketing company that studies the subconscious processes that drives consumers to buy. The CEO, Indian-born K. Pradeep, has developed an electroencephalogram or EEG, which is a skullcap device containing sensors that capture synaptic waves. By using this cap and capturing brain data, the company collects information on buying from consumers across the world. The difference, between this company and the consumer marketing focus groups of the past, is a study of the neuroscience of the subconscious buyer. It's a science that picks up electrical signals from the brain, sending them to analyzation software. The data is subconscious and unfiltered, so it isn't corrupted by beliefs.

This is a big breakthrough for the power of neurosciences and understanding what makes us tick. Neuromarketing is a big thing for corporate America, when it comes to increasing share and gaining the advantage. Why shouldn't you capitalize on the power of your own subconscious mind as well?

If corporations are doing it, it's certainly a process that will change the way you think. Let's tap into that 90 percent of your brain that's not being utilized. It's possible that you've been seeing only what's in front of you, reacting to what you see, and ignoring subconscious drivers.

Your Subconscious Beliefs

There are a diverse array of views and assumptions when it comes to the study of happiness and positive psychology. A positive mood is easy to obtain. I could go now and get a hot dog and be happy. I could get a massage and feel really happy, or a drink of wine and feel instantly giddy. But the happiness we are talking for the purposes of this book is a sustainable feeling of contentment and satisfaction, versus a temporary feeling of exuberance. Excitement and adrenaline are one thing; raising the GNH (Gross National Happiness) is a global, worthy cause that can transform generations for years to come.

We are tapping into happiness at the root of your being. The subconscious level is the DNA of who you are, and the foundational property of how you think.

In true, sustainable, subconscious-driven happiness that we are focusing on here through the see it, say it, move it, prove it process, the change is like a waterfall of positive process geared toward the future, not the past. This means that, in order to be progressive and move forward, you must eliminate the old toxic behaviors of the past.

Remember when we talked about hitting the telephone poles? In a prior chapter I wrote about how some people hit the poles while driving because they were so focused on it. This is called target fixation. It's a concept fighter pilots often report being sucked into during missions or training missions, when their aircraft ends up in a downward spiral. Target fixation is dangerous. When you get so completely focused on one thing, you can lose sight of every other thing. Lamar Smith, CEO of First Command Corporation and the author of *There's More to Life Than the Corner Office*, was a former fighter pilot who was well-versed in target fixation. He wrote about how this one thing can damage every other thing in our lives. If we are fixated on one specific thing to the detriment of everything else, our lives are in danger. I would add to that theory. Not only your life, but your family and your legacy.

And, you can lose sight of reality.

There are generally perceived societal myths about happiness that you may have bought into without realizing it. For instance, if you ask a young person about their life, most will tell you they expect to be happy when they're old, yet many old people believe they were happier when they were young. Both groups believe dementia and physical decline set in beyond a certain age and it all goes downhill from there! Why do you suppose people believe that? Is it because of what they see? Sure, the majority of elderly people are in failing health these days, but the majority of Americans young or old, according to statistics, are in debt, obese, and facing divorce. But that doesn't have to be you! You don't have to be part of the majority. Ask a large section of the population and you'll find that both the younger group and the older people expect to become less happy as they age. This is a foundational societal belief.

But remember the centenarians (rare individuals statistically!), don't believe that way. They haven't bought into the lie that life is less happy as you age. They probably don't spend a lot of time dwelling on thoughts like that. They know that every season brings new things, new people, adventures, and places.

Happiness Is a Key Factor in Longevity

When you are flexible and willing to learn new things, your brain and body are healthier. The process you've learned here in this book will allow you to see it, say it, move it, and prove it. When stressful moments occur in your day, week, or year, you'll be able to quickly and subconsciously interrupt the pattern and move on.

What do the happiest people in the world know that others don't?

As of this printing the oldest reported living person in the world is super centenarian Besse Cooper, a 115-year-old retired teacher in Georgia who always loved the outdoors and working in the garden. When she was interviewed she had a positive outlook and humorous view of life. Live happy! I promise you'll enjoy your life more, and longer. We can learn a lot about people who live beyond 100 because they seem to have varied interests and a willingness to learn. Other centenarians have included Tom Spear, who at 102 still played 18 holes of golf three days a week, and Nora Hardwick, who still drove after 100. Centenarian Audrey Stubbart taught Sunday school, and still worked 40 hours a week as a reporter and columnist for her local newspaper. York Garrett at 101 still worked every day as a pharmacist in North Carolina. Dr. Ralph Foster practiced chiropractic work in his home office at age 98, still seeing patients weekly, and Helen Small wrote her first book at 91, got her MBA, and landed a new job in the aging division of a major Texas hospital in Dallas.

The secret to longevity includes a positive attitude! It's not olive oil, or a geographical cluster on a remote island that leads to long life. It's a combination of factors, including an ability to be happy despite stressful influences around you.

I'd venture to say that not many centenarians keep up with the constant barrage of electronic information in the world. I doubt they're linked up to Facebook from their iPhone. In fact, most centenarians interviewed live simple lives and consider it unremarkable that they've reached 100. They're happy just for the sake of being happy. According to the global centenarians blog based in the UK, "The remarkable things about these centenarians is just how unremarkable they consider themselves and their lives to be. As a group most centenarians seem to be very humble. Most dismiss living to 100 as being in and of itself any kind of achievement, but say any life no matter how long or short carries with it its own rewards if it has been a life well lived."

Guard Your Heart (and Mind!)

Your heart and mind are your most valuable assets, like precious natural resources of oil in Saudi Arabia, or gold to a miner. You wouldn't let a bank robber into the vault if you were the manager of a bank, so why let someone in to steal your biggest asset? Guard your heart from toxic emotions and your mind from destructive thoughts.

Throughout the process that I've been teaching you, it is important to remember that you can control a lot of what comes in, which will help to prevent the negative or toxic from automatically flowing into your brain. It's simply being aware of what you're allowing in and living life intentionally. Since your mind is the doorway to your heart, start being aware of what goes in it. Remember the movie *The Yes Man*? Jim Carrey played a character who literally said yes to everything. No matter what it was, he said yes. It seemed like a positive thing but it ended up getting him into trouble and costing him a lot. Don't buy into the lie that information is power in a society where everyone is talking and twittering about nothing, 24/7. Maybe information is just information. Sometimes information is garbage. Eliminate the garbage and detox and become happier.

Detox from Information Periodically

Our world has exploded with information. Look at the world's most dominant companies and you'll see that the ones we use each and every day are all about the sharing and dissemination of information. Google has 1,000,000 servers, and 24,000 employees. Facebook operates behind the scenes with 60,000 servers and 2,000 employees. Yahoo has 50,000 servers and 13,900 employees bringing you information daily with just one click.

Much of the time we are subconsciously making decisions as we click through emails and see ads in our peripheral vision, and it places a Post-it note in the brain to buy later. Later, at the store, this Post-it note memory is recalled and you stand at the checkout and buy. Other times we seek out direct information, such as when a home buyer searches for houses on Realtor.com or a car buyer searches Craigslist or the Internet classifieds for a vehicle. But even while we are doing all this direct searching, there are indirect messages coming in. We live in an age of too much information. We are over-informed, over-stimulated, and over-marketed to.

Knowledge might be power, but it can also lead to an overload of your nervous system if you can't make an intentional decision to stop, interrupt negative input, and maybe even fast from information for a few days. People fast from food in a process to cleanse their liver and other organs, giving their digestive system a break.

Some people I know take a deliberate information technology fast, shutting down the computer and phone for a week. In that process of cleansing, you strengthen and sharpen your ability to hear.

Happiness Is Global

When I set out to write this book, after decades of helping people all over the world get happy, my publishers wanted to make sure we focused on the global aspects of happiness, in various cultures. I've worked in Finland, Russia, Singapore, Brazil, and beyond and I can tell you that it isn't about economics, but about the other factors that reside in the mind. The truth is, economics aren't the driving force behind happiness. Happiness is intangible and hard to define because happiness is a state of mind.

Who are the happiest people in the world?

I say that the happiest people in the world are the ones who choose to be.

Chapter 13

LIVING YOUR LIFE WITH INTENTIONALITY

"He gave the world another world."
—*George Santayana, on Christopher Columbus*

» **THINK INTENTIONAL THOUGHTS**

» **CREATE INTENTIONAL OUTCOMES**

» **CREATE A NEW INNER WORLD**

Steve walks with a limp, lumbering awkwardly down Main Street in Dallas, Texas. He's clearly homeless, his black tennis shoes worn full of holes. The shelter gives Steve a thin mat to sleep on, on the cold concrete floor just inches away from hundreds of other homeless men, all lined up in rows, and huddled, shaking beneath their own jackets. In the morning, the men are forced out into the air, or, if they prefer, they can stay in a holding area in the shelter, sitting at tables.

Steve prefers to venture out onto the street. He walks out into the sunshine with a metal cane, and rests occasionally at a stop sign to catch his breath. From the outside, he might appear to look like just any bum down on his luck, after being laid off. It's hard to recover from a major economic setback when you can hardly walk. But when you talk to him, your perspective shifts.

"I used to be in a wheelchair," Steve says, smiling joyfully. "But it went in for repair and they never gave it back. I kept calling, and calling. Finally I just decided not to sit around anymore."

He holds up his cane, and the bottom legs where rubber stoppers once were, are all worn down to the metal. "You can see I've been doing some walking!" he says, laughing. "I bet I walk ten miles a day, and I've lost weight!"

When I was in his situation I wasn't as evolved. I let myself get bogged down in negative emotions. But Steve, on the other hand, has a positive mental attitude about his situation that makes each day a gift. Encountering him, you feel blessed to have what you have, but astounded that there are people like him in his world.

Studies on post-traumatic stress disorders show that even victims can rebound after a tragedy. This is worth mentioning at this point in a book like this. Because victims of all kinds of traumas and horrible crimes, from war to witnessing deaths, to experiencing rape or emotional abuse, report major emotional growth following such traumas.

Let Go, and Live Happy!

Letting go of traumas and being able to adopt a new mindset about your future is the key to living out the rest of your life in a happy, productive state where you find joy and abundance and give back to others. If you've had tragedy in life no one can overcome it but you. But when you do overcome you'll be stronger, and able to mentor others.

Mercedes Ramirez, a young girl who survived one of the world's most significant commercial airplane crashes, is now an inspirational speaker who helps people discover their second chance at life.

When the accident happened Mercedes was buckled up inside the cabin of American Airlines flight 965, holding her father's hand. It was her twentieth birthday, and the last thing she remembers was switching seats on the airplane, so that she could sit beside her father and watch an in-flight movie. It was *Die Hard*, an action flick featuring Bruce Willis. The college student was exuberant about the trip. Her parents had promised to take her to their native Colombia to see the tropical nation for her birthday, and the time had come for an exciting adventure! It was December 20, and the airplane cabin overflowed with families traveling on holiday. Brightly colored wrapped Christmas packages were stuffed into the overhead bins, and in the rows ahead, children laughed. The movie turned on, and that was the last memory she had.

Days later Mercedes and three other passengers were rescued, broken and bleeding, from the top of a mountain in Buga, Colombia, where the airplane crashed. The pilots, flight attendants, her mother and father, and everyone else on board died. Everyone except Mercedes, a young man her age, and a father and his young daughter. Mercedes was one of only four passengers to survive more than twelve hours in a remote jungle with extensive injuries.

I use this true story of resilience as an illustration that humans are magnificent, resilient, wondrous creatures, yet sometimes we just don't know it. But deep inside we have the ability to transform, just like the mythical transformer toy robot your kids used to play with, that can be one thing one day and another entirely different thing another day. Today Mercedes is an author and inspirational speaker who travels the world (by plane). Like Anthony Robles and the others we've mentioned in this book, she was encouraged to greatness, despite her circumstances.

Dr. Richard Tedeschi is a leader in the study of happiness and well-being after trauma, and in his findings he analyzed post-traumatic growth. Dr. Tedeschi is professor of psychology at the University of North Carolina at Charlotte, where he teaches personality and psychotherapy. As a licensed psychologist specializing in trauma, he found that many people do bounce back to effectively give back, recover, and raise levels of happiness within themselves. Happiness is a choice. And by interrupting negative patterns, you can make it an ongoing, simplistic, subconscious one.

Remember, what you focus on is what you get. You've been armed with the information and education you need right now to work this process. Now is the time to change your life. See it, say it, move it, and prove it! Be magnificent!

When I was speaking to a large audience at a workshop in Finland, which once had one of the highest suicide rates in the world, I noticed that the Finnish people were quite reserved. They were even more reserved than the English audiences I'd addressed. Various cultures have different tendencies and personalities, and while a crowd in Brazil would naturally tend to be laughing and loud and boisterous, others like the Finnish, would not.

But one thing that struck me during the exercises I was teaching them is the way the Finnish seemed to crave happiness. They were low key and hard to get engaged, but once you got them engaged and active in the exercises they didn't want to stop! They wanted to stay full-on in the happiness and the process. It was an interesting experience. And the government of Finland over the past decade worked tirelessly educating the people in their country about ways to overcome depression, decrease stress, and get happy! Today their suicide rate has declined by 40 percent, all because the country was intentional about educating people about the mind, and changing its culture.

Intentionality Is the Key to Most Successes

If for the next ten days you're intentional about getting happy, you will be. Repetitive, consistent intentionality is the key to losing weight, changing a relationship, studying for an exam. Whatever it is you strive to achieve, do it with focus.

For the next ten days find at least two times a day that you can rehearse your Further Faster Happiness process. You will be doing ten repetitions of the process each time. This should take you no more that five to seven minutes to complete. Then move on with whatever it is that you want to do.

If you are doing two sessions then ideally do them as close to the time that you get up and as close to the time that you go to bed. Accelerate the process by increasing and doing three and even four sessions per day. As this goes on you will find that it will become increasingly harder to remember and feel the negative feelings.

Have fun with it! See it, say it, move it, and most of all prove it. Anything is possible, and it's time to become the magnificent creature you were created to be.

YOUR HAPPINESS ACTION PLAN

From your study, remember:

- » Happiness can be learned
- » Happiness speeds up success
- » Happiness will increase your energy
- » Happiness will increase your longevity
- » Happiness attracts you to what you want and what you want to you
- » Happiness increases your health and wellness
- » Happiness is contagious
- » You can condition yourself to be habitually happy

There's an important link between your body and mind when it comes to happiness. Toxic emotions create stress, impacting overall wellness. The truth is: You are not stuck with the state you're in now. If you're unhappy, you don't have to be.

The Happiness Process

Step 1.   See it
(see and feel the negative).

Step 2.   Say it
(say your key word to interrupt the pattern).

Step 3.   Move it
(move your body to widen the gap
and prepare the nervous system).

Step 4.   Prove it
(stimulate the positive emotion
and place it in the gap).

Step 5.   Groove it
(praise and repeat; do it over and over again).

First, block out at least ten minutes where you can be alone and undisturbed. Find a quiet place where you can make some noise without anyone interrupting. It might be a closet or a bathroom. It might be somewhere outside. Eliminate media. Turn off phones, televisions, computers, and anything that could distract you. Be willing to be silly and have some fun!

Second, choose a key word to interrupt your pattern. It can be anything that causes you to shift your focus and arrest your feeling. Make it fun and even silly. You can say "hello," "wait," "wake up," "love," or even "pizza" or "cake." Anything! So long as it is strong and different. If you are having a hard time coming up with a key word, just use "STOP." And, it is okay to change your key word later, just use the same key word all the way through each session before changing it.

Step 1.   Stimulate the un-resourceful feeling. While in a
seated position briefly imagine the feeling that you
want to replace. It can be the same as the feelings
that you wrote about in Chapter Four. It was the

thing that stops you and hinders your progress in terms of happiness and feeling good. You can also just imagine yourself unhappy. It is not necessary to feel it deeply, just the beginnings of it. The first time is the longest but as soon as you feel any part of it (*this will bring forth the negative*), then…

Step 2.   Abruptly say your key word out loud. You can even shout if you feel so inclined. The more radical the better. (*This will temporarily interrupt the negative thought and emotional pattern and obliterate the feeling /pattern and create a scotoma.*)

Step 3.   Immediately jump to your feet, shake your body out, and take a deep breath (*this will widen the scotoma and create a mental vacuum*), then…

Step 4.   Put the biggest smile on your face, snap your fingers and say the word "MAGNIFICENT" out loud. (*You will have stacked up several happiness anchors that will fill the void when you fire off the anchors in that moment.*) Because your brain and your nervous system were forced to operate in a vacuum, they will be searching for something to fill that gap. This is where you will be inserting your new happy and positive feelings. And because you have built them up from the past, they will come quickly without you having to search for them. It's way cool!

Step 5.   This last step in the process is what I call "Groove It," which is simply celebration with praise. When you praise yourself, you lock yourself into

the process of thinking differently. Do a little
dance, make a little noise, get down tonight.
Shake your butt, pat yourself on the back, and
say something cool to and about you like "I
freakin' ROCK!" (my personal favorite).

Repeat steps one through five 10 times. Each time you will
notice that it will be harder and harder to feel and bring up the
negative.

Your future literally lies in your own hands! So just do it!!

The 10-Day Happiness Action Plan

First gather these things:
  » A timer (cell phone, alarm clock, etc.)
  » Get some great music and find songs that
    make you smile and feel happy

Then schedule your Happiness sessions on your calendar. Use
your smartphone calendar if you can. I like digital because it will
remind you through an email or a chime that it is time to do your
daily exercise. Think of this like brushing your teeth. From this day
forward, it's part of your routine. If your chime goes off when there
are people around, you can still go into a bathroom and do it! It's
about a daily routine and the compound effect of building positive
thought. You wouldn't miss brushing your teeth, so don't miss this!

Here Is Your Schedule

For the next ten days find at least two times a day that you can
rehearse your Happiness Process. Ideally, the first time should be
within the first two hours of your waking up. Don't start your day
with this as you will be starting it with the next piece, but just make
it within your first couple of hours of the day. You will be doing ten
repetitions of the process each time. This should take you no more

than five to seven minutes to complete.

Try to do the second set of your Happiness Process at least an hour and a half before you go to bed. The reason for this is that a great deal of the time you will find that you have a lot more excitement and energy when you are finished with the exercise and it might hinder your ability to go to sleep. People tell me all the time that they feel so good and are so excited that they can't get themselves to sleep right away. You'll find this great to do during the day if you suffer from the midday drag.

If you are like me and you want to really accelerate the process then you can do three and even four sessions per day. As this goes on you will find that it will become increasingly harder to remember and feel the negative feelings. But this is only part of the results. You will also start to notice other things like better disposition all around, greater peace and confidence, less stress, and more ambition and drive. Your energy and thought patterns about the world will change, because your role within it has changed. You're in the driver's seat, and you're choosing to live happy.

Smile, Remember, Breathe, Praise

Now, set your timer to go off every two hours after your morning Happiness Process. When it goes off, stop whatever it is you are doing and put a ridiculous, huge smile on your face. Remember as many things that you are grateful for or happy about. (Even if you have to make it up at first you will soon find even the small things will come to mind.) Take five deep diaphragmatic, slow breaths and then praise yourself for doing the exercise. Then reset your timer again for two hours and get on with your life.

Recommended Reading

Allen, James: *As a Man Thinketh*. First ed. 1903; rev. ed., Tarcher, 2008.

Bormans, Leo: *The World Book of Happiness*. Firefly Books, 2011.

Hill, Napoleon: *Think and Grow Rich*. First ed. 1937; rev. ed., Random House.

Lechter, Sharon L.: *Outwitting the Devil: The Secret to Freedom and Success*. Sterling, 2011.

Maxwell, John: *Winning with People: Discover the People Principles That Work for You Every Time*. Thomas Nelson, 2005.

O'Kelly, Eugene: *Chasing Daylight: How My Forthcoming Death Transformed My Life*. McGraw Hill, 2005.

Robbins, Anthony and Joseph McClendon III: *Unlimited Power: A Black Choice*. Simon & Schuster, 1997.

Smalley, Dr. Gary: *The DNA of Relationships*. Tyndale House Publishers, 2004.

Acknowledgments

A great team makes everyone stronger.

Many thanks to the committed group of individuals who made this work a success. Stuart Johnson, Dr. Richard Deeley, Jim Rohn, Doran Andre, Reed Bilbray, my literary collaborator Tammy Kling, Steve Jamieson, Tony Robbins, Sam Georges, Matthew Bennett, Loren Slocum, Sage Robbins, Andy Broadaway, Donte Andre, Paula Pecorella, Virginia Smith, Dr. John Oda, Steve Linder, Lisa Jannette McClendon, Anita Joy McClendon, Mo Hanslod, Mike Keonigs, and all of the team and staff of SUCCESS Books and their parent company Video Plus.

Most of all, I honor my beautiful family. Tina and Joseph, you are my guiding light.

Notes

1 Population Reference Bureau: "Today's Research on Aging." No. 17, June 2009.

2 Rowe, M.D., John Wallis and Robert Kahn, Ph.D.: *Successful Aging*. Dell, 1999.

3 Achor, Shawn" "The Happiness Dividend." Harvard Business Review, June 2011.

4 McClendon, III, Joseph, *Change Your Breakfast, Change Your Life*, Abundant Press, 2008.

5 The Gerontological Society of America: "The Palisades: An Interdisciplinary Wellness Model in Senior Housing Study." Oxford University Press, January 2011.

6 Achor, Shawn: "The Happiness Dividend." Harvard Business Review, June 2011.

About the Author

Joseph McClendon III is a global leader in the peak performance field. As an instructor at the University of California (UCLA), Joseph taught re-engineering, leadership, management, and advanced communication courses for the Engineering and Management Extension program. His company, Pro-Sequences Research Group, is a leading peak performance coaching organization that works with leaders in the political, entertainment, and business communities. His commitment to give back and assist others in achieving happiness within themselves has been the driving force in his career.

Joseph holds a doctorate in neuropsychology and several certifications in the neurosciences, and is an expert in life transformation by assisting others in overcoming fears, phobias, and emotional challenges. His remarkable ability to go straight to the core of the challenge and effect rapid change makes him a unique commodity as a turnaround specialist and success coach for the more than three million people worldwide he has taught.

Joseph has authored two books with world-famous peak performance coach Anthony Robbins, including the bestseller *Unlimited Power: A Black Choice.* As the senior head trainer for the Robbins Research International he has worked side by side with Anthony Robbins for over two decades, training individuals and teams. His story and messages have been featured in many national magazines, including *O Magazine*, *SUCCESS*, and *Success from Home*.

He lives in Southern California with his wife and son, Joseph McClendon IV.

   www.MakeYourFate.com

   www.facebook.com/JosephMcClendon

R e s o u r c e   G u i d e

Unlimited Power: A Black Choice

In their national bestseller book, Anthony Robbins and his longtime associate and friend Joseph McClendon III address the specific needs of African Americans in search of knowledge, courage, success, and a better quality of life. Available at www.amazon.com.

Change Your Breakfast, Change Your Life

Learn the simple truth about how we all function as human beings. Making just a few simple changes in what you do first thing in the morning will stimulate your body and mind to produce more energy, health, better emotions, enhanced appearance and more. Available at www.MakeYourFate.com.

Putting a S.T.O.P. to It

The S.T.O.P. technique is a powerful yet simple system designed to arrest negative/disempowering feelings and memories that fuel negative behaviors and replace them with more powerful emotions and behaviors that propel you further faster. Audio program with workbook.

The True You

In just 10 days, you can create more powerful confidence and greater self-esteem! This simple step-by-step system trains you to automatically produce stronger self-image. Take control of the words and images that you think that trigger outstanding feelings and behaviors. Audio program with workbook.

Go to www.SUCCESS.com for more information.

SUCCESS®

What *Achievers* Read™

Your monthly supply of new ideas, inspiration, and resources that will continue to give you the competitive advantage in life. Each magazine comes with a SUCCESS CD, featuring interviews with Darren Hardy and today's greatest achievers and leading success experts.

www.SUCCESS.com/subscribe

SUCCESS®
BOOK SUMMARIES

SUCCESS Book Summaries provide a sneak peek at the content of each featured book, with a special focus on chapters that resonate with entrepreneurs and achievers. With a subscription to SUCCESS Book Summaries, you'll receive summaries of three featured books in printed, audio, and PDF formats each month. By reading and listening to the summaries, you'll know whether the books are titles you'd like to add to your personal success library. Listen, read, and achieve more!

www.SBSummaries.com

Go to www.SUCCESS.com for more information.